AF505399

# Afraid of the Dark

# Afraid of the Dark:
## What Suffering Tells Us About God

by
R.P. Nettelhorst

# Quartz Hill Publishing House
Publishing arm of Quartz Hill School of Theology
*Quartz Hill, California*

Quartz Hill Publishing House
43543 51st Street West · Quartz Hill, CA 93536
www.theology.edu
info@theology.edu

# Table of Contents

## Chapter One: The Question

The question of why bad things happen to good people is a question that is directed at a particular someone: God. And inherent in the question is blame. "Why did *you* let that happen to *me*? Couldn't you have stopped it? You're the almighty creator of heaven and earth. Couldn't you have done something? Couldn't you stop the pain, the agony, the loss? Why did my baby have to die?" Our query is not unreasonable.

It's also at the heart of what is sometimes called "the new atheism" in the bestselling books by Sam Harris, Richard Dawkins, Christopher Hitchens, Victor Stenger, and others. Of course, calling it the "new" atheism, is a bit of a misnomer, since it's what has driven atheism for a long time. Voltaire submitted the same question back in the eighteenth century in his book *Candide*.

From the horrors that fill both our histories and our memories, the atheist recoils and concludes that either God is a sadistic son of a bitch, or that he doesn't exist at all. The atheist has decided that the best explanation for the world as it is, is to believe that there is no one to believe in, no one to put one's trust in, no hope, and no future: God does not exist. There is no one out there that cares. And that's why bad things can happen to good people.

Are atheists right? How can we answer their—and our—agonizing howl of *why?* What does suffering demonstrate about God? What does pain tell us about who God is, how he relates to his universe, and what our expectations are?

The better we understand God, the easier it will be for us.

### Life and God

*Yea, though I walk through the valley of the shadow of death, I will fear no evil: for thou art with me   (Psalm 23:4 KJV)*

This is what life is like.  We are all walking through the valley of the shadow of death.  Bad things are going to happen to me.  If they are not bad now, just wait.  If they *are* bad now, just wait.  Back and forth we go, like a ping-pong ball.

The problem of the ultimate question, the question of suffering, is that our emotions are in play.  We are not just thinking about an intellectual, academic issue. We mostly don't approach it with cool, clear logic.  It is personal.  Our guts are fully engaged.  We too often have tears in our eyes.

We get mad when our expectations are not met.  That's part of the difficulty in our relationships in general.  We go to a fast-food restaurant.  We order a strawberry milkshake.  Then they tell us they are out of strawberry, but they can give us a chocolate shake.  We get angry.  Because our expectations were not met.  Our *reasonable* expectations.

When something bad happens to you, and you get mad at God, the reason you are mad at God is because he didn't meet your expectations of what he would do for you.

But consider a possibility: that our expectations of God are out of whack.  Who we think God is, what he has to do for us, how he has to behave—could we have misunderstood something?   It would be ludicrous, for instance, to go to a bookstore and then get mad because we couldn't buy a new set of golf clubs.

We need to worship the God who is, not the god we wish for, not the one we made up in our heads.  If we are mad at God, perhaps the problem is that we don't know God as he actually is.  We might be mad at the god we made up in our mind.  In which case, we need to stop believing in our made-up god and find the real one.  Then we won't get mad at the real God.  The real God won't disappoint us. The real God won't tell us that we can have a strawberry shake when he knows there aren't any there. There won't be any bait and switch with the real God.

The characters portrayed on the pages of scripture sometimes get mad at God.  They accuse God.  But that's because they had expectations that weren't accurate. They'd made something up in their head about God that wasn't so.  We all do it, and we all do it all the time.  We need to work at minimizing that.  We'll probably be happier if we ever can.

Humans are not as rational as we'd like to imagine. Most of the time, it is our emotions that drive our decisions, and then after the fact, we justify it rationally.  Sometimes we do okay and come up with good, logical reasons.  Not always, however.  And this one question regarding the reason for suffering, this ultimate question, is particularly problematic in that respect.  Emotion is almost the only driving force in the consideration.  And so we can't ignore that.  This question rears its ugly head in the worst possible moments of our lives, when we are raw and untethered and beside ourselves in tears and pain and grief and horror.  It is the question we ask in the hospital, by gravesides, in the midst of holocausts.

All the platitudes offered as kindnesses by the well-meaning drive me crazy in the middle of the maelstroms. All I want to do is lash out at those who try to comfort me with clichés that are meaningless in the moment.  Unless you can heal my child or raise the dead, you cannot help me when the unthinkable happens.

But the mind-numbing storm of grief is not permanent. What we will discuss in these pages probably won't make the grief any better when it crushes you. It will, when the storm clouds fades, perhaps help you gain perspective and understanding: in the calm that comes much, much later— in a year or two or five.

### Searching for Answers

Not all problems have easy solutions.    Not all questions have easy answers.

But we *like* easy answers.  We prefer simple solutions.

And the atheist answer is an easy answer: suffering means either that God is malevolent, or that there is no God. The standard Christian answers are easy answers, too, and all too often, equally useless and bogus: such as the suggestion that bad things happen to you because God is chastising you. Repent, you sinner!  Job's friends liked that answer. Much as we'd prefer that the solution for a broken ankle be a few dabs of essential oils, rather than months in a cast and a year of physical therapy.

Sometime a simple answer is just flat out wrong. There is much wrongness to go around on this topic of suffering. A huge amount.

Part of the problem is that there is so much baggage to unpack.  On Facebook I will regularly come across some bit of nonsense and I have to decide if it is worth the effort to try to correct it.  Usually it isn't.  It takes too much effort and it won't be effective anyhow, because most people don't really want the truth, they just want their beliefs reaffirmed.  Narrative trumps truth for most people.  Again: we are remarkably unreasonable creatures.

To fix stupidity I have to go to a lot of work: there is a lot of stuff people think is so that I have to show isn't so. Before I can even begin to correct the mistake in the Facebook meme, I have to fix a lot of underlying, unstated assumptions on which it is built, along with all the weird presupposition and various untruths that they believe besides that.

Crackpots will write a book and then trumpet "no one has refuted me!"  That's usually because the experts in the field think the crackpot's ideas are so insane that no one could possibly take them seriously since they are obviously wrong.  But to refute a crackpot's book isn't easy, even for an expert. Usually it takes another book to undo the one by the crackpot. For instance, my senior project in college was to refute the crackpot concept of British Israelism. This led me to write a very lengthy, two-part magazine article. But the complete refutation required me to write an additional 50,000 word thesis.

This is what we face in approaching the question of suffering and what it says about God. We have *a lot* to unpack.

So let's get started.

But first. Perhaps I should give you the answer. Then, over the next few chapters, I can explain the answer. What I say now may not make a whole lot of sense. If it did, we wouldn't need to spend any more time with the topic.

Since the answer is not as simple as we might like, we will have to move through it slowly and do some heavy lifting, in order to bring us all up to speed, as it were. I call the explanation the three L's:

1. **Logic**. Logical fallacies are common errors in reasoning that will undermine an argument. At first glance, such arguments may seem to make sense, but if we examine them closely, we soon realize they lack evidence for what they purport to claim. Both atheists and theists are remarkably adept at using a particular, very common, logical fallacy in regard to this issue of suffering. It's called "*agumentum ad ignoratum.*" The Latin phrase simply means "argument from ignorance." It's like pointing and asking me "what is that odd creature?" but when I shrug "I don't know" your response is to insist "then it must be a unicorn." The fact that I don't know the answer to your question does not mean that your proposed answer must be right.

If scientists don't know the explanation for a process, as Christians we like to say "see, God did it." And if an atheist asks a question that we don't know the answer for, he will say "see, there is no God." Atheists say that suffering demonstrates there is no God because Christians can't explain why there is suffering. Christians will look at questions like, what caused the Big Bang, and when there is no obvious answer, proclaim, "see, God did it."

The atheist and the Christian, in so responding to "I don't know" with their favored responses are equally wrong. Your opponent's failure to have an answer to your question does not make your answer right.

2.    **Liberty.** "Time and chance happen to all," writes the author of Ecclesiastes (9:11). The universe appears random, and there appears to be freedom. This suggests that God has allowed freedom and has chosen to allow for an "open" universe. If so, then he governs by freedom rather than micromanaging. He therefore appears to prefer liberty to totalitarianism. God has then both chosen to limit himself, and in fact, is limited in what he can do. He cannot be absurd: one and one always equal two; they will never equal forty-seven. God cannot make one and one equal forty-seven any more than you can. It is something he cannot do. He cannot sin. *Et cetera.* Suffering tells us something about God. We must define—that is—*understand* God accurately.

Demonstrating that dogs are not green does not mean that there are no dogs. *Demonstrating that a certain sort of "god" does not exist is not the same as saying "there is no God at all."*

3.    **Leftovers.** For the universe to exist, it must be asymmetrical, that is, there is imperfection inherent in it. Without imperfection, there would be nothing: a pearl cannot exist without its inner sand grain. The universe would not exist, we would not exist, if everything were perfect. At the moment of the Big Bang, there was not an exact balance of matter and antimatter; there was, instead slightly more matter and we exist because of that. Planets do not orbit in perfect circles; they orbit in ellipses. Our bodies are bilaterally symmetrical, but not perfectly so: our

hearts are not in the exact center of our chests, our faces are not exactly the same on both sides. And so on. Suffering means the world is not perfect. That does not mean the world is not good.

### Suffering is Universal

A comedian once did a standup routine about white privilege, and how being a middle-class, straight white male meant that in the game of life, he had gotten the equivalent of a Royal Flush. If his life was a video game, it was set on the easy mode.

But of course, the whole concept behind our modern notion of inherent privilege based on external factors of skin color, ethnicity, or gender is ultimately nonsense.

As Ecclesiastes tells us:

In this meaningless life of mine I have seen both of these: the righteous perishing in their righteousness, and the wicked living long in their wickedness. (Ecclesiastes 7:15)

And:

I have seen something else under the sun:

The race is not to the swift
or the battle to the strong,
nor does food come to the wise
or wealth to the brilliant
or favor to the learned;
but time and chance happen to them all.

Moreover, no one knows when their hour will come:

As fish are caught in a cruel net,
or birds are taken in a snare,

so people are trapped by evil times
that fall unexpectedly upon them. (Ecclesiastes
9:11-12)

It's not just our outsides that determine if we have "really" suffered, or "really" been privileged.

My great grandfather on my father's side was a sharecropper. He was working in a field with a bunch of other sharecroppers one day and one of the people working with them was Black. The other sharecroppers refused to eat with him. My great grandfather did, and told the others, who criticized him for doing so, "if he's good enough to work with me, he's good enough to eat with me."

My family on my father's side may have had it better. My grandfather was an engineer, but during the depression, he was a prison guard. He also had a farm.

My father, born in 1932, remembered when, as a boy, his family first got electricity. He told me spent a lot of time flipping the light switch on and off, fascinated by the wonder of it.

His older brother fought in the Pacific during WWII and shot down kamikazes trying to crash into his ship. My dad made a career in the Air Force and went to Viet Nam twice, before retiring after 28 years as a chief master sergeant. Later he worked as assistant athletic director at a small university in Ohio for 20 years or so.

My parents were able to pay my way to college, but then I had to pay for my graduate degree by working forty or more hours a week driving a shuttle bus at an airport parking lot while taking sixteen units, all in ancient languages. Somehow I managed to learn more than a dozen dead languages over three years while averaging four hours sleep a night. At the same time I dated and married my wife. Later I taught some college classes, wrote some books, and wound up as a pastor of a small church.

Since my wife and I were infertile, after ten years of marriage we fostered three little girls and one little baby boy, who died of SIDS.

We adopted all three girls. Two have serious mental health issues.

So, struggle and suffering is a part of my experience. We *all* suffer, no matter our genders, our sexual orientation, our ethnic background, our skin colors. Suffering does not discriminate. It is not wise to get into a contest over who is the bigger victim, who has suffered more, or who is more privileged.

Pain is pain. The two-year-old crying over spilt milk or a stubbed toe—his suffering may not seem like much. But he's only two.

Again: this isn't a contest.

We all have pains: some private, some public, some hidden, some open, some obvious, some not.

Pain is the topic at hand, together with its implications. What effect does it have not only on how we live our lives, but on our very understanding of God, who he is, how he works, what he expects? Suffering impacts our day-to-day existence, and our understanding of self, others, and the divine.

Modern atheists, at least from the time of Voltaire, reject God and deny his very existence. They feel anger at him—the one whom they believe is non-existent (how you can be mad at someone who doesn't even exist is an interesting psychological puzzle in itself)—primarily because of the enormity of suffering, both their own, and their disappointments with life and living, and with what they see in the world around them. The agony of the world is so overwhelming it leads them to decide that the very existence of such horrors precludes the possibility that there could be any sort of God at all. They have decided that God and misery cannot both be part of the same reality.

*Star Trek V* is not the best of the Star Trek movies by any means, but it has its moments. Over the course of the film, Spock's brother Sybok uses his Vulcan abilities to take the pain from various individuals.  He offers his service to Captain Kirk.  Kirk rejects the offer. He says, "You know that pain and guilt can't be taken away with a wave of a magic wand. They're the things we carry with us, the things that make us who we are. If we lose them, we lose ourselves. I don't want my pain taken away! I need my pain!"

That is profoundly inciteful.

## Chapter Two: Moving Toward the Right Question

The author of Ecclesiastes writes:

> I have seen something else under the sun: The race is not to the swift or the battle to the strong, nor does food come to the wise or wealth to the brilliant or favor to the learned; but time and chance happen to them all. Moreover, no man knows when his hour will come: As fish are caught in a cruel net, or birds are taken in a snare, so men are trapped by evil times that fall unexpectedly upon them. (Ecclesiastes 9:11-12)

So do these words in Ecclesiastes mean that you can do everything right, be a good person, follow all the rules, and your life can still go to hell in a handbasket?

Yes.

On any given morning a whole lot of people will get up and eat their breakfasts. Some will kiss their spouses and head off to work. Some will beat their spouses. Some will beat their kids. There will be people who get up, take a deep breath, shower and then go out and murder someone, or have an affair, or embezzle money, or lie. On any given morning there are those who have been up all night drinking and using drugs and having unprotected sex with people they aren't married to. Some people will be laughing, some people will be crying. Some people will be doing what they are supposed to do and some will not. Some are good Christians. Some are bad Christians. Some are not Christians at all.

But three thousand people out of the six billion on planet Earth one bright September morning went to work like they always did, a day no different than any other, but they never came home again.

Terrorists chose to fly airplanes into their workplaces that particular day. Were they greater sinners than all the other people on the planet? Ordinary people and the terrorists who murdered them both died on the same day, from the same cause.

Bad things can happen without warning and without reason and it isn't because God is mad at you or loves you less than those who didn't suffer that day. Consider these words from the New Testament:

> Now there were some present at that time who told Jesus about the Galileans whose blood Pilate had mixed with their sacrifices. Jesus answered, "Do you think that these Galileans were worse sinners than all the other Galileans because they suffered this way? I tell you, no! But unless you repent, you too will all perish. Or those eighteen who died when the tower in Siloam fell on them—do you think they were more guilty than all the others living in Jerusalem? I tell you, no! But unless you repent, you too will all perish." (Luke 13:1-5)

When you're driving down the freeway and traffic slows in front of you and you put on your brakes to stop, is it your fault when the person behind you doesn't and plows into the back of your car? Of course not. You may drive carefully. That doesn't make your neighbor drive carefully. Were you a worse sinner than the driver in the lane next to you who went on unscathed? How about that crack dealer who was beating up his girlfriend a block away?

### A Nightmare Come True

Three thirty on one cold January morning I was awakened by the sound of a baby crying. I was exhausted, having been asleep maybe four hours, and already short of sleep from previous nights of getting up to take care of Derrick. Derrick was our six month old foster baby, the brother of our two year old foster daughter, Brittany. I did not want to get up, but Ruth, my wife, was tired too, and so why not? In not the best of moods I staggered to the kitchen and found the formula, put the ingredients together, shook, heated the bottle, and then got Derrick out of the cradle at the foot of our bed.

I checked his diaper, changed it since it was a little messy, and then gave him the bottle, which he sucked down slowly, over the course of a half hour or so. When he finally finished it, he was still fussy. I tried putting him back down in the cradle at the foot of our bed, but he was not happy there. Then I tried the swing, but the rocking wasn't giving him joy either. Finally, I set him on the couch in our living room, and to my pleasure, he finally sighed and scrunched up, apparently comfortable at last.

Good, I thought—and managed to make my way back to my bed, where I fell asleep almost at once.

Seven o'clock. The TV popped on in our room and the *Today* show had begun; the lead story was the news that Sonny Bono was dead from a freak skiing accident. Ruth was still half asleep, and I rolled out of bed, thinking I should go check on Derrick and see how he was sleeping.

Arriving in the living room, he was still scrunched on the couch; I walked over to him, peered down at him, and felt a chill. Looking more closely, I failed to discern any movement. I put my hand on him. Nothing. I picked him up, and he flopped, totally unresponsive.

He wasn't breathing!

But that couldn't be. Why wouldn't he be breathing? What in the world? I tried patting him, but nothing. I began undressing him, thinking maybe that would revive him, wondering what could be wrong. I began yelling for Ruth, "Something's wrong with Derrick." I tried blowing into his nose and mouth, beginning CPR, and feeling scared to death.  Ruth finally came out, and she immediately took him in her arms and started yelling at him to wake up, then she continued the CPR on him.

I hurried into my home office and called 911.  "My baby's not breathing!" They assured me that paramedics were rolling and would be there right away.

After I hung up, I called our private agency social worker, and our county worker and let them know what was up.  Within five minutes, the paramedics were coming through the door.

Ruth had been screaming at Derrick between giving mouth to mouth and compressions; now that the paramedics arrived, they took over and asked me to help Ruth out of the room.  While they worked, we stood in our library hugging each other.  Eventually, they called Ruth and I back in, and we made the decision that Ruth would ride with him in the ambulance.  After Ruth and Derrick had gone outside to the ambulance, one of the paramedics came to me and told me that it didn't look good, that he was in bad shape.  I just nodded and said "I understood, I know"...and then they were gone and I made my way back to the office and started calling people.  I called our friends Kathy and Dandi and our pastor.  I let them know that Derrick had stopped breathing, that he was probably dead, and that Ruth was going to the hospital in the ambulance and they could meet her there.

It is hard for me to remember all the details, the order of events; everything seems jumbled.  I remember feeling empty, but knowing that I had to maintain and get certain things accomplished, like calling the people that needed to know.  Kathy showed up at some point, I remember, vaguely.  I think she was there when Ruth called and confirmed that Derrick was dead.  It was about 8:30 AM.  I remember seeing Kathy sort of slump against the wall when I told her.

I had our other children, Toni and Brittany and Vanessa to take care of, to feed. I explained to them what was going on as best I could, trying to adapt the news for them, though for Toni and Brit, there was really no way to make them understand. Vanessa didn't go to preschool that day. At four years of age, she understood something had happened, and she knew Derrick was dead. She had come out of her bedroom when Ruth was working on him. But I really can't remember what I said, now, except that I was concerned with doing it carefully, keeping it at a level she could understand, making her as comfortable in the midst of the turmoil as possible.

At some point Ruth and Pastor Don and others were back at the house. We were concerned about contacting Derrick's grandmother, because she was scheduled to pick him up for a visit at ten that morning and neither we nor the social workers had been able to get a hold of her. And so it fell to us to break the awful news to her when she arrived at our door. Ruth drove her to the hospital then to see Derrick's body and Don and Dandi went with them, too, as I recall. I remember being in a fog, feeling empty, feeling hardly anything at all, actually, except a vast gulf of isolation. I didn't know what to do, to think, to say: I was simply existing moment by moment.

Our private foster agency social worker told us that the other children, Toni and Brittany (who were only our foster children at the time), would probably be removed from the house, at least until the investigation was over. Maybe Vanessa, too, even though her adoption had been finalized by that time.

And so we waited, wondering when it would happen, trying to pack bags for them, trying to let them know that they might have to go away for awhile, trying to hold them and caress them and comfort them and ourselves as much as we could while we waited. I felt empty, empty, empty and completely alone.

At three that afternoon, we finally got a phone call telling us that the girls were not going to be removed from our house after all.  Our county social worker had talked to her supervisor and convinced him to let our girls stay with us.

Late that afternoon, the social workers and their supervisors arrived.  We related what had happened, telling them all that we had done, gone through, showing them where he was, how he had been sleeping, and the sequence of events.

And they tried to reassure us and comfort us and let us know that it wasn't our fault.

I remember a house full of people that night and I kept telling everyone who came that we didn't expect them to be able to say any words that would make anything better, but just the fact of them being there, staying with us, keeping us company, was what we needed just then.  Merely to sit and be with us, without even speaking a word was enough.  And I was pleased and marveled at the fact that all the people were there, and how they were swarming around Ruth and helping her and comforting her; and I was concerned, above all, at trying to make her as comfortable as possible, to ease her through the pain.  But I remember thinking to myself, as everyone was there, and the focus was on Ruth—I remembered wondering what was going to happen to me; was there going to be anyone there for me, to help me, and I decided that I just had to do what I could to help Ruth; if she was okay, then I would be okay.  I would survive, I would endure, whatever happened.  And I would see to it that Ruth was okay.

But I felt so alone; I kept wondering where God was, not in the sense of "why did this happen?" or "why didn't he stop this from happening?"  I did not question God's wisdom and purpose; I knew God, and I knew that he had a reason for what was happening.  My question was, *why do I feel like I'm alone here?*  Why don't I feel God's presence, why don't I feel his arms around me, why can't I feel okay? How long am I going to hurt like this; how long can I endure wondering if my children are going to be taken from me? So they haven't taken them yet. How long before that changes, before someone, somewhere decides that "action must be taken?"

At last, everyone had to leave, we had to be left alone, it was time to go to bed. Our children were asleep, and now it was just the two of us. All I remember, in trying to sleep, was lying in bed, under the covers, in a heated waterbed and shivering uncontrollably, feeling cold as ice and not being able to get warm. Sleep was intermittent, unsatisfying; I don't remember dreaming at all. And every time consciousness came, I wished that it could just all be a nightmare, that I would wake up and it would not have happened after all. I've had really bad dreams like that, where I would suddenly awake, and the relief was so enormous, so wonderful...and I longed for that feeling but it wouldn't come. After a long while, morning arrived. We had to face another day.

We had determined to try to maintain a schedule, to make sure that Vanessa got back to preschool; of course, we told her teacher what had happened, since we didn't know how the trauma of what had occurred the day before might affect her.

And then, the time passed; people came over again, though not as many. They spent time with Ruth, and I tried reading the Bible, and didn't receive any comfort from it, but I read it anyhow, and reminded myself that like the song, "when I don't see you, I know you're there, when I don't feel you," and so on. I understood, that as alone, as empty, as hopeless, as fearful at the potential loss of my other children, that even though I felt nothing, couldn't see or explain or understand what was going on, still God was there. He said he was; and I didn't doubt it, but I still couldn't relax or feel any comfort. What I wanted more than anything was to feel at peace, but instead, I could feel nothing.  I felt alone; I didn't feel anything from God, or from anyone else for that matter.  I didn't know what to say, or really where to turn or who to turn to.  All I could do was pray, read the same paragraph over and over again in the Bible, seemingly never quite remembering what I had just read.  I had heard stories of people going through dark times, and telling how they felt the presence of God with them; but that was not my experience at all.  I was alone, with only the cold promises of the Bible to cling to, and the experience of my life up to that moment.  And that was going to have to be enough, I decided, unless God chose otherwise.  I prayed over and over that he *would* choose otherwise.  But, I knew, perhaps this emptiness, this sense of being alone, was something God needed me to experience, too.

But as the day wore on, I found a slight shifting occurring; I managed to find some sense of comfort in a passage, and shared it with Ruth and it seemed to help her, which made me feel much better.  And our children were still with us, which was a miracle in itself, and I recognized the hand of God in how events were playing out.  That helped some, and yet...inside, I felt a gap, a disconnect.  And I found myself reassuring people around me that I didn't expect them to be able to give me an answer, or press a button and make me feel better, but simply that their presence, their concern, was what really counted. But, dear God, how I wished that someone could have found a word, a phrase, a verse of scripture, *anything* that would make me feel better.

This second day, as I recall, we took the girls to the doctor to have them checked for a particular respiratory virus that was going around; we were concerned that perhaps that had been what had killed Derrick since he had been slightly congested. Meanwhile, we were awaiting word on the autopsy, which would tell us exactly what had happened to him. The two most likely causes were either this infection, or a case of SIDS (Sudden Infant Death Syndrome). Of course, we also worried that maybe they'd find something else anomalous, and wondered if they could twist some innocuous thing into some form of abuse, and blame us and accuse us of mistreating him in some way. We awaited the results with a lot of trepidation. I tried to divert myself by reading; I read three of Robert Asprin's books from his *Myth* series. They were funny books, and I actually was able, for a few moments, to distance myself from what was going on. I remember, through those next days, what seemed endless interviews, and visits by social workers and phone calls. We feared the supervisor people coming out, and we still wondered how long before they would take our girls from us.

I got to where I just wanted the bad feeling to go away. I had previously scheduled a board of Trustees meeting for that Saturday for the Quartz Hill School of Theology, and so I left for that at noon, still awaiting word from the coroner over what exactly was the cause of death. I have little memory of the meeting, aside from getting the impression that everyone was somewhat distracted and didn't seem to really notice or care. Couldn't they tell how bad I felt, how miserable I was? Why didn't anyone try to comfort me, tell me they felt bad for me, hold me or hug me or something? Where was everyone and why did I have to be alone?

About a week later, when we finally got the results of the autopsy, we felt enormous relief. It was now confirmed SIDS. Sudden Infant Death Syndrome meant that it had not been our fault. There was nothing we could have done, nothing that we did do. The social workers were relieved, too; it confirmed for them their faith in us, and ratified their decision to leave our children with us.

With the autopsy report in, that meant that Derrick's body could now be released to the mortician. His biological family had Derrick cremated and the funeral was scheduled for that week; I do not remember the day of the week; perhaps Tuesday. The biological grandmother asked us if we could get Don, our pastor, to do the funeral, and asked us to pay his expenses, which of course we agreed to.

The biological grandmother gave Don very explicit instructions about what to say during the funeral, and of course he followed the family's wishes. A lot of the people from our church attended; in fact, at least half of the people there, perhaps more than half, were members of our congregation. My parents sent a large flower arrangement, and several other friends and family members also sent arrangements that were arrayed in front of the funeral parlor when we arrived.

A tape of rather poor quality through a bad sound system played in the background. Our pastor gave the eulogy. He spoke at length about how much the biological father cared for Derrick, and how close he was to him, and what a great loss his death was. Pastor Don talked about the grandparents, the biological mother, and other relatives. Ruth and I were not mentioned at all; we had known ahead of time such was to be the case. Don was upset by our exclusion, and several church members later expressed dismay that we had not been mentioned or allowed to participate at all.

The biological father had said a few words; I don't remember them. I can't remember what songs were being played, either. Derrick's biological mother hadn't been able to attend at all. She was in prison.

We expressed our regrets to the family, and so did many of the members of our congregation. This was the last time that we saw the biological family that they were even marginally civil with us.

**Keeping Our Children**

After the funeral, all the bio family's attention was suddenly directed toward Brittany.  This was dismaying, but not unexpected.  Still, we had to question the sincerity of their motives, considering that they had ignored Brittany for months at a time, and that the biological grandmother had never even met her until that December, about fifteen months since she'd been born.  Now, suddenly, the grandmother was claiming to want to have custody of her.

The court hearing that followed soon after the funeral was devastating.  Although they left Brittany in our custody, for the time being, they ordered an investigation into whether we smoked in our home (despite the fact that we were nonsmokers), among other things. As the judge said, "we know secondhand smoke can contribute to SIDS".  Additionally, they gave biomom's sister and the grandmother, three-hour unmonitored visits with Brittany.  Until then, only the biological mother and father had been allowed to see her, and then only once a week for a one hour *monitored* visit (which they had very rarely ever managed; the first eight months we had Brittany, she had received absolutely no contact with the biological family: not so much as a card or a phone call).

After that court date, our private agency social worker called us into her office and told us that we needed to hire an attorney; she told us that Brittany was a lost cause, and that she'd inevitably go back to the biological family; but Toni was another matter, and so a lawyer would allow us to shore up her status so it would be very difficult for anyone to remove her from our home.  As just foster parents, all it took was the word of a social worker and the child would be gone.  But if we got the special arrangement known as de facto parent status, then it would take a judge's order for the child to be removed, and then there'd have to be good cause.  The special arrangement was a precursor to adoption; it essentially told the court and the state that we were intending to adopt Toni, and so she was bound more closely to us.

So we contacted the two lawyers that our social worker had recommended; we ended up going with the cheaper one, who charged only $125 an hour instead of $250 an hour; his retainer was only $2500 instead of $4000, and my parents were happier to give us the smaller loan.

I remember feeling an emptiness inside, a gnawing sense of futility, like trying to slog uphill in hip-deep mud. But I also believed that God knew what he was doing. I just wasn't sure I was going to *enjoy* whatever it was God was doing, but I knew that whatever happened, God loved these children more than I did, so whatever he chose was going to be the best thing possible. But I knew that it might still hurt me an awful lot. A shot is not a pleasant thing, but sometimes it is the best thing; that's how I looked at it.

So, the biological mom's sister picked up Brittany one day for a three-hour visit; she arrived a bit late and brought her back a little early. She smelled slightly of smoke, which bothered Ruth and I, and of course we documented it; we were writing down everything that happened.

The biological grandmother also picked up Brittany for a visit, and she was as regular as clockwork about it. We were convinced that the next time we had a court hearing about Brittany, that we'd lose custody to her, and that would be the end of it. I felt horrible every time I had to open the door and let that woman carry Brittany away; it was as if she was ripping my arm off, spending the day with it, and then reattaching it later, but knowing that someday soon it was going to get ripped off again, and sooner or later, it wouldn't be coming back.

The next court hearing on Brittany was set for March. Just a couple of weeks before then, while our private agency social worker was doing her weekly visit in our home to check on the kids, the phone rang. I picked it up and someone on the other end told me that the biological grandmother had just suffered a heart attack. I thanked the person for letting me know, expressed condolence and a wish that she'd be okay, and then I hung up the phone.

I was happy; even ecstatic. Because I knew at that moment that Brittany *wouldn't* be going anywhere now: not with the grandmother's health being that fragile. I came in and told the social worker, and she stared at me with a shocked look, not really knowing what to say. I asked her if she'd heard of the German word, *schadenfreude.* She hadn't. I told her it meant taking secret delight in the misfortunes of your friends. She half-smiled, but didn't say anything more.

Proverbs says that we shouldn't rejoice when we see our enemy stumble, but I found it very hard not to; and I talked about the fact that I found it hard not to be pleased. And, it seemed to me, and to Ruth, I think, that this was the hand of God. We had the grandmother added to the weekly list of prayer requests at our church, but frankly, it was hard to pray for her. To be honest, at least in some place inside me, I really would not have minded if she had died. I felt guilty for thinking that; but I could not bring myself to sincerely pray for her recovery.

The next court date in March went very well for us. Instead of moving toward reuniting Brittany with her biological family, the movement now was toward terminating the biological family's rights and a hearing was scheduled to do just that. Despite our social worker's assurance that we were going to lose Brittany, suddenly, we found, in only a month's time, everything had turned back around to our favor.

I was starting to breathe again, at least a little bit. With Toni, everything was going smoothly; her biological mother had dropped out of the picture, never made it to any of the court dates, and so we got our special de facto parent status. Not too long after that, they terminated the biological family's rights and so we moved from foster care with Toni, to being officially in the adoptions process with her.  Surprisingly, with our own private attorney working for us, the adoption proceedings went much faster than they had with Vanessa.  He expedited things, and told us his goal was to get her locked in with us as fast as possible, so we could then focus attention wholly on Brittany without distraction.  Thus, very soon, we had officially adopted Toni.

In the meantime, we and our pastor arranged for a memorial service for Derrick.  The service was for us and for the church members, since everyone had felt so dissatisfied with the funeral.  Also, we invited our social workers to come to the memorial service, since the biological family had explicitly asked that they not come to the funeral.

And so, we had our memorial.  It was a lovely service, but I find I can barely remember what happened, or who was there.  I remember there were more people there than we normally had on a Wednesday night, and I remember that people came by and prayed over Ruth and I.  But my thought in going through the memorial service was that this was for the church and for our social workers, because they'd been deprived of a real funeral, and this would give them good closure.  I didn't feel anything much myself; I didn't think that it was something that I really needed, and I remember looking forward to the event with great discomfort.  But I survived the evening, though I didn't seem to feel anything from it.

As the court hearings came, and the objections, and the delays went on and on, it was becoming increasingly certain that Brittany would be ours.  And yet, every hearing was a nightmare to me; I dreaded the getting up early in the morning, the long drive, the interminable wait in the big waiting room.  The grandmother never appeared at another hearing after her heart attack.  But the biological parents tended to be regular, which of course added to the stress of the whole situation. Of course, the biological mother was still in prison, and so she was only in the courtroom, never in the waiting area. And the biological father didn't always make it. But my stomach was always in knots, and I was always uncomfortable. I would take books with me to read, and I would open them and stare at the page, and my eyes would move over the words and I didn't seem to ever be able to remember anything; I found myself going over the same paragraph the whole time, getting absolutely nowhere.

What I was feeling was fear. I was afraid that the judge would decide that Brittany shouldn't live with us anymore. And despite the fact that I knew that God knew what he was doing, and despite the fact that I knew he loved Brittany more than I did, I still thought it could happen that Brittany might go back to them. How could I know that Brittany being with us was God's will for all of us? I'm not God, I don't know the full picture of reality, the place where all the threads of history were going to go. What seemed really bad to me, losing Brittany, might in the long run be a great good; I couldn't tell. But knowing that whatever happened was going to be for the best, did not make the knots in my stomach, the anguish in my heart, or my terror go away. The bad feelings stayed. I wondered what the peace that passes all understanding could possibly feel like; I imagined it would feel good, that somehow in the midst of this turmoil and stress, I would magically be serene. If that's what the peace that passes all understanding is like, then I never felt it through this whole mess; I'm not sure if I've ever felt it—*if* that's what it's supposed to feel like.

Once we got de facto parent status on Brittany, things proceeded smoothly enough; the most stressful court date after that was when parental rights were terminated. We waited outside the courtroom for what seemed like forever. We had arrived at a little past 8:00 AM; court always opened at 8:30, and we had to be there then, regardless of when they would get around to putting us on the docket. None of the biological family for Brittany were in the waiting area, and our lawyer arrived a little late. But once he was there, it wasn't very long before our case came up. When you have your own lawyer that you're paying for, they put you at the top of the docket, we discovered. When we walked into the courtroom, the biological mother was there, but the biological father was not. She was dressed in orange prison garments, and as I recall she was wearing chains. The judge read through the purpose of the hearing, and then took statements from the counsel. The biological mother's court appointed attorney announced that the biological mother objected to the proceedings. The judge seemed hardly to be paying attention to anyone. Unlike in TV dramas, in real life judges mumble, talk fast, and its pretty much all monotone. With a few words, the judge simply announced the termination of the biological family's parental rights, and the placement of Brittany into adoptions.

The long battle for Brittany was suddenly over. And we had won. Despite every indication from our social worker, despite all that had happened because of Derrick, not only had none of our children been taken from us, we now knew they would never be. Brittany was ours.

Our private agency social worker, especially, was ecstatic; she really found it hard to believe that things had worked out the way they had. Of course, with parental rights terminated, and Brittany moving into adoptions, we were technically no longer foster parents and she would thus, at the end of the month, cease to be our social worker. Instead, we would simply have an adoption worker.

Our private agency social worker continued to maintain contact, of course; and wanted to know when the adoption was going to be finalized.

One item of stress hung in the backs of our minds, though. That was the fear of a lawsuit. Our primary concern up till this moment had been adopting Toni and Brittany. With Toni safely adopted, and Brittany now in adoptive placement, the fear of losing our children was finally eliminated. But we had known, on top of that stress, the stress that we were likely to be sued for wrongful death in the case of Derrick.

One thing that we had tried earlier, before the termination of parental rights, back at the early part of the year, was to get both the biological family and us into a counseling situation, where an attempt at reconciliation, and working through the anger issues could be accomplished. Our attorney thought that maybe, if the court ordered counseling, and with some non-disclosure agreements, and maybe even some agreements not to sue, that we could avoid any possible future legal action.

So, the court had ordered us and the biological family into counseling; and Ruth and I made one trip down to see a psychologist. His office was in a strip mall, not too far from a Subway restaurant. It was a nice office, and he was very nice, too. And I told him about my biggest fear in all of this: losing our children. He just kind of nodded, and listened and didn't say much; he didn't seem to ask a whole lot of questions. It was over in an hour and we left.

We understand that the biological grandmother met with him at least once, too; but it wasn't too long after this that we got the first communication from an attorney hired by the biological family: two envelopes, one addressed to me, one addressed to Ruth. They held identical papers: a Tort claim.

In a panic, we called our lawyer and faxed copies of what we had gotten down to him; he calmed us a bit by saying that we hadn't been sued yet; the papers simply gave the biological family the right to bring suit later, if they chose.

So, we continued with our day to day lives, getting up in the morning, feeding the children, getting Vanessa off to school and Ruth off to work; meanwhile, in all these ups and down since Derrick's death, I would make my way to my office and sit down in front of the computer and stare at the monitor and try to find something to write. Since Derrick had died, I had found it impossible to write a book. I had started five the first year after he died, but I could never get more than a handful of pages in; if I got thirty pages over a month, I was doing well. I tried to rewrite, and found myself doing a lot of staring at the page, reading the same paragraphs over and over and not being able to make much sense out of them. Slowly, bit by bit, maybe a few pages at a time, I progressed.

In frustration, I threw myself into doing work for the School of Theology. I created the web pages for the classes. I tinkered with the look, the layout of the different web pages. I tried to find new and creative things to put on the site, links I could make to other sites of similar interest.

I found that nonfiction, oddly enough, was easy enough to write, and so I focused on writing essays on theology. I suspect that the reason nonfiction was easy to do during this period was because academic nonfiction doesn't require so much in the way of emotional effort. Writing a novel has been described as an easy process: you just poke a vein and start bleeding on the paper. Well, my veins all seemed to have collapsed. One of the few pieces of fiction I managed was a short story on gluttony; of course, even that was more theological than purely emotional. Even so, it was very hard for me to write, far harder than fiction usually is for me, or was, before Derrick died.

I spent a lot of time working at my church. I knocked down walls, built an office, built shelves, and catalogued 7600 books for the library. The needs of the School of Theology kept me very busy; but I found it very hard to focus even so.  Only mindless activities like cataloguing books could I do; building things I could do.  But paperwork was always a struggle.  I found it very hard to grade tests and papers; I was always wanting to put it off.  I found it hard to do administrative tasks, such as writing letters, working at setting up board meetings, or even preparing for accreditation once one of the board members had loaned us the money to pay for that.

And I was increasingly uncomfortable with publicizing the school, for fear of publicizing me.  I knew that with Derrick's death and a potential lawsuit pending, that it was somewhat surprising that the newspapers or other media hadn't picked up on it.  In fact, one of the scariest moments one morning about a year after Derrick's death came when one of the local newspapers called—and they weren't just trying to sell me their paper.  They wanted to ask me about Derrick, and about being named in a wrongful death lawsuit.  I told them no comment, and got off the phone as quickly as possible.  And then I called our lawyer and let him know what had just happened.

He told me to never give news media any information.  I was instructed just to always say "no comment," and then to direct them to his office.

Our private agency social worker called shortly after that, having gotten a similar call; she was as confused and frightened as I was.  We didn't know what to think; neither we nor private foster agency had even been served yet.

Our attorney told us to not make it easy for them; stay out of sight; keep the blinds down; don't answer the door unless you knew who it was.  Our private social worker said that sometimes they'll call and then hang up without saying anything, because they just want to find out if you're there, so they can serve you the papers.

I was terrified.  But then, there was just silence after that. Nothing more happened.  We got up in the morning, got everyone off to where they needed to be, and I sat down in front of the computer.  I spent every morning after that opening the paper in sheer terror, reading carefully, certain that I was going to find my name.  I did searches on the newspaper's website, looking for the story.  But there never was any story about Derrick or us, and searches on the web never brought up my name in any context except the School of Theology.  And yet, I had this fear weighing on the back of my mind, not always really consciously there, but there nevertheless.

And every quarter, I had to send out a press release to announce the new class schedule, so that we could let people know what we had to offer, so that they could come and take classes from us.  And I was petrified that sooner or later, the newspaper would want to interview me about the school.  So I was very careful to leave any mention of my name out of all the press releases.  When I was inducted into *Who's Who in America*, I avoided sending out any press releases on it; there was no way I was going to publicize myself.  If I became in any way a public figure, then the whole thing with Derrick would become a big media circus—or so I feared.  I even stopped writing letters to the editor.  I didn't want their attorney to see my name anywhere and think to himself, "hmmm, maybe I can exploit this..."

But after that one phone call, and the two letters about the Tort Claim, there was nothing.  No summons were served, no more calls from the media, and then, suddenly, we had a court date: Brittany's adoption would be finalized in June.  We immediately went into celebration mode, preparing a party for the adoption, sending out invitations.  Both our private and county social workers were planning on coming to the party.  They wanted very much to see this thing happen, this thing that had seemed so unbelievable only a few short months earlier.  And even as we celebrated, even as we relaxed, I still, in the back of my head, knew that there was something unpleasant coming.

We had a good time with the celebration after Brittany's adoption.  Everyone came and visited, enjoyed the food, and chatted; our county social worker brought us a rose bush; our private social worker came, too, and actually seemed pretty cheerful.  I don't remember much in the way of details.

In any case, we got a last little bit of paper work from our lawyer, and a letter telling us that since the threat of a lawsuit seemed to have faded and seemed unlikely at this point, that we could just relax and enjoy our lives with our children and focus on taking care of them now, at last.  We could put the stress of the past year or so behind us and move on.

Happily ever after?  Had we finally reached that tomorrow, that place of paradise in our lives, where the air would forever be sweet, the hole in our life filled?  Did we now live in paradise?  Of course not…

**Piling On**
A pleasant enough July afternoon: my friend had come over for some instructions in using a computer. That, and I think she just liked to come over and talk on occasion; she certainly had enough stresses in her own life and I always felt at such a loss as to what to suggest that she should do. In any case, she was over, playing on the internet and my children and hers were playing in the living room.  I was not thinking about a whole lot at that moment, beyond listening to make sure that the kids were all right, and trying to pay attention to my friend and whatever it was that she needed me to do at the moment.  Ruth was gone for the evening at Magic Mountain with our foreign exchange student from Spain.  Karen and Amy, teenaged daughters of friends of ours, were temporarily living with us, too; it was a rather crowded and busy time, just then.  Just before five, the doorbell rang and I went to answer it.

A young man dressed in a white shirt and wearing black shorts smiled, dropped some papers in my hands, and informed me that "I have a bit of paperwork for you." And then he quickly turned and disappeared.

I looked down at what was in my hands, but I already knew what it was. The summons had come at last. Just when we thought maybe, just maybe nothing would happen. Boom. Here it was. And goody, I'm all by myself. Ruth is gone, and there's no way I can get a hold of her. She won't be home until after ten at the earliest. Oh well; I knew what I needed to do. I told our visiting teenager Karen to get off the telephone *now*; I was rather abrupt and harsh about it I'm afraid, but I really didn't care. I was upset and she happened to be in the way of the first thing I absolutely, positively had to do immediately, and whatever she was doing at the moment on the phone really didn't matter; certainly not as much as this. And so, the phone clear, I called our attorney. Of course, he was busy, and so I left the message with the person who answered, identifying myself and telling him that we had just been served with a wrongful death lawsuit over Derrick.

Then, that done, my friend was staring at me. Her eyes told me she was terribly disturbed by the news, but equally, she didn't know what to say any more than I knew what to say about it. I decried the fact that Ruth wasn't around and that I couldn't tell her, but I thought it was just as well that she could enjoy herself this evening and not have to worry about it.

"So what are you going to do?" my friend asked.

"Well, I've got a deacon's meeting tonight; I guess I'll go to that if someone can watch the kids..."

"I can do that."

"Thank you."

I don't remember much of the rest of the conversation we might have had; I remember staring at the papers, going through them, and becoming increasingly agitated. Our attorney finally (really, it wasn't very long) called me back and I gave him the details; he told me not to panic, and to fax a copy of the papers to him, which I then proceeded to do right away.

And thus, the legal battle commenced. He told me he'd file the necessary preliminary responses, and he'd be nosing around, and he'd let me know, of course, what was happening.

It was frustrating; we had just finished paying off the bill for Toni and Brittany's de facto parent status, among other legal things, and the adoptions, amounting to over four thousand dollars. Now we were staring at who knew how big an expense. Of course, our lawyer told me not to worry about that, the state had a fund to protect foster families in just this sort of thing, and that maybe our homeowner's insurance would cover the legal expenses. Thus began a long and frustrating series of phone calls and letters that in the end netted us absolutely nothing in the way of financial help.

The deacon's meeting that night consisted of our pastor and my fellow deacons Rex and Sherman; I don't know that anyone else was there that night; perhaps Rick was there, too. It is oddly disconcerting to find the gaps in my memory. I should be able to remember more of the details. What I do remember, however, is what I was feeling, and I was feeling numb; devastated; empty. I was at a complete loss and really didn't know what to expect now.

I shared a bit with Don before the meeting started, and so whatever else may have been on the agenda before, my problem suddenly became preeminent; I laid the summons on the table in the library and I remember staring at it the whole meeting, occasionally picking it up, feeling it, and putting it back down. I don't remember much of what was said; I don't remember what was prayed, though I remember that everyone prayed; well, everyone except me—well, out loud that is. I just sort of moaned a bit at God, wondering in essence, okay, what now? I know there's a purpose here, and I know you know what you're doing, but gee whiz, this is really, really awful and I don't like it one bit and I wish it would just go away.

So I went home after the meeting; I don't remember what anyone said to me, although I'm sure they were talking to me about it. I drove home; my friend was still there. I put the children to bed; my friend stayed until Ruth got home a little bit after ten. I do not remember the conversation we had while we waited. I am sitting here, trying to see myself back in my office, and I'm pretty sure most of the time we were in the office, but I don't remember the words; I just remember that my friend looked very sad.

Ruth finally got home, and after the initial exuberance of her return, and separating her from our exchange student, I put my arms around her and told her that I had some bad news. And then I showed her the papers and told her that we'd been sued for thirty-one million dollars. Also named in the suit were the County, our local hospital, our county social worker, and our private foster agency.

Her reaction was to explode: "how dare they do this!" And then she said that the biological grandmother could "kiss her visits with Brittany goodbye now." Up until then, we had allowed the grandmother to take Brittany for three hour visits once a week. Brittany seemed to enjoy them, and we thought it would be good for the grandmother and help her with her grief over Derrick; now, we began to see the whole affair up to this point in a slightly different light. The biological parents were the named plaintiffs in the lawsuit, and legally the only ones who could have brought such a lawsuit, but it was unlikely that they would have had the financial capability of bringing a lawsuit like this on their own.

I slept badly that evening; I always sleep badly when I'm stressed: my mind simply refuses to relax or shut down at all; instead, the thoughts just go round and around. I think through what has happened, what might happen, what would be good if it happened, what would be bad if it happened, and it goes off in sometimes unrelated directions. Occasionally, in such a state, I get up and try reading my Bible and praying for a while; sometimes that helps. I don't recall if I wound up doing so that night or not.

The next day, Ruth called our lawyer and discussed with him the situation with the grandmother. He agreed that there were no good reasons to continue letting her see Brittany; she had no legal right to see her in the first place; her visits were purely at our discretion; and there were now obvious sound reasons for terminating the visits. She was likely to become a witness and it would not do well to have her around where she could spy on us and Brittany and concoct any manner of thing against us. Not that she was likely to do any harm to Brittany, or try to kidnap her, but, the visits should end.

I had mixed emotions about terminating the visits. The grandmother had always seemed pleasant enough; she called me "daddy" around Brittany. And yet, I knew for certain that her politeness and pleasant words had not been honest in the least and that she was a hazard now, and in fact for some while had been a hazard, both to me and to my family. So, Ruth called her and told her the visits were over, and told her why. The grandmother feigned shock at the size of the claim against us, though she admitted to knowing about the suit.

I had very unkind words in my head when I heard that. However, I don't think I actually uttered the words out loud.

Still, the grandmother asked if she could phone or send cards, and so we agreed to that. She also asked for a last one-hour visit in our front yard, to say good bye to Brittany, and so we permitted that as well.

I was the only one home when she came. The grandmother parked her white van in front of our house and sat with Brittany by our tree while I watched from the front door. I felt angry and worried, wondering at every moment whether she would do something. But she did nothing, and brought Brittany back up, and mouthed something about regretting the situation, and I said something innocuous back instead of wishing her a quick trip to Hell. But in my head, I did not think nice things. Afterward, with Brittany safely back in my arms and the grandmother gone, I hugged her tightly and told her I loved her more than anything, and told God that I knew I shouldn't have thought those mean things about the grandmother and to forgive me. I'm unclear if I genuinely repented, however. And I know that the imprecatory psalms, those psalms where the writer asks for the violent destruction of his enemies, became good reading for awhile after that...

And so now I had a new storm cloud to hang over my head. We'd just had the annual used book sale for the School of Theology, and we were disposing of the unsaleable books. As I was helping load the books that we were not going to use in the future into the back of a pickup, I talked with those helping me about my nice new lawsuit; and of course we chuckled over the thought of them ever getting thirty-one million dollars out of us, and I told them that my lawyer had assured me that we could always claim bankruptcy anyhow and they'd never get a cent from us. But I didn't like the possibility of them getting a cent out of the County, either. I knew that this was about money, and nothing but money. Their hope, I was convinced, was that the County, rather than going through the expense of fighting the lawsuit, would simply pay them off.

As things developed, however, the County was in no mood for paying off on this one. They chose to fight it, and so did everyone else named in the suit. This was a comfort, in a way. It signaled to us that their case against us must be weak; of course, our attorney kept telling us that they had no case at all. Nevertheless, the lawsuit was always on my mind, oppressively.

I remember a couple of incidents. Once, shortly after Derrick had died, within a day or two, I had to go to the grocery to get some milk. Standing in line, looking around, I noticed carefully all the people going about their normal affairs, and I wondered if any of them were suffering as much as I was at that moment. And then the clerk, as he rang up my order, asked me, "and how are you tonight." I briefly thought about replying, "oh, just fine. My baby died yesterday, but otherwise, no problem." But of course I simply answered, "fine." and he took my money and I left.

And now, with my newly-sued status, I went to the same grocery store and had similar thoughts all over again; and of course, I just answered "fine" this time, too.

The suit was served against us on a Monday; or it might have been Tuesday; I really can't remember now. But I do remember the prayer meeting that we attended right after. We laid the lawsuit on the pulpit and prayed to God about it. Doubtless there were those in the legal profession who would have been appalled that we shared with our church everyone what was going on. But they were our family. What else could we do?

Things were busy for the first few weeks. We faxed things back and forth, signed faxed documents, sometimes signed documents that were sent in the mail to us. Eventually, our response was filed (it had to be filed within thirty days of being served, and of course we made the deadline). And then, things were quiet for a little while, until a big fat envelope came from our lawyer holding something called Interrogatories. They are part of the discovery process the plaintiffs use in an attempt to find out all the bad things about us that they could. Many of the questions were innocuous, like name, date of birth, place of residence, and the like. Some asked questions about what we had done with Derrick the previous month, week and twenty-four hours before the "incident"; Ruth had a set of questions, and I had a set of questions. We had to answer details about his medical history, how often we had taken him to the doctor, when, and for what. They also made accusations, wanting us to admit to doing things that we had not done. Our attorney, whom we of course called, explained how to answer the questions, what the point of it all was, and helped us through it. We finished them all, and mailed and faxed everything back to him, and signed where we had to sign. A few weeks later, he sent us copies of the official legal format of our answers. They were worded much better and much more precisely now. Additionally, our attorney responded to many of the interrogatories with an objection, arguing that they had no right to be asking us that particular question. It looked impressive and made us feel a bit better.

And then, I got the lovely letter telling me that I was to be *deposed*. This was scheduled for October, in the other attorney's office; I was told in the letter that I needed to set aside the whole day, and to be prepared for having to come back again the next day and maybe even more after that. I also had a list of more interrogatories to answer. Oddly, they seemed virtually a repeat of the previous set. But, I dutifully answered them and got them back to our lawyer in the time allotted. I hated answering the questions; I did not like doing it, did not want to do it, would have refused to do it if I at all could; it knotted my stomach and stole sleep from me. And now, I had to go to this attorney's office and have him grill me? I was not looking forward to this at all. In fact, I was dreading it. It was hard not to think about anything else. My only comfort in the whole thing was the thought that at least they hadn't asked Ruth to do it, although our attorney thought she'd probably be next. In fact, he was a bit surprised they hadn't asked her first.

And then, a day or two before it was scheduled to happen, I got a phone call from my attorney telling me that their attorney's secretary had called to postpone the deposition.

The relief I felt from that news was enormous; but, of course, as Ruth reminded me, it was *only* a postponement. Doubtless it would be rescheduled. My attorney told us that these things happened, and that it would probably be rescheduled within the month. So, I immediately went back to being stressed.

Our private social worker called me the night before the deposition had originally been scheduled, telling me that the foster agency's attorney was going to be there, and wishing me all the best. And I got to inform her that it had been postponed. She was shocked, wondered why, and I of course had to tell her I didn't have a clue.

For a month, I kept expecting with every ring of the phone, to hear my attorney's voice telling me the deposition had been rescheduled. Every time I got the mail, I expected something in there telling me the news I was dreading to hear. Every time I checked for messages on the voice mail, I had that fear in the front of my brain. And nothing happened. Ever. The deposition was never rescheduled. In fact, no depositions were ever taken from Ruth or me. As the months passed, the fear of that deposition finally faded, at least a bit.

But, of course, the paranoia that became my life remained. Our neighbor told us once that he had seen a car parked in front of our house with a couple of people in it for a long time. And then when he went to go talk to the people, it drove off. I began to wonder whether or not they might have hired a private detective to watch us. Every time I got in the car, sometimes consciously, sometimes just as a nibble on the back of my neck that I tried to brush away, I wondered if someone was following, watching where I was going, what I was up to. Were they peeking into my windows when I wasn't around? Were they shaking their heads over my dirty swimming pool? Were they examining my financial affairs and chortling over the difficulty we were having making ends meet each month? I wondered if they were disappointed by the fact that they kept finding me making my way over to the church rather than having some affair somewhere or frequenting prostitutes or spending my nights in a bar. Would they see me that time when I yelled at Vanessa, or got cross with Toni, or snapped at Brittany? Would some innocuous action be taken out of context and used against us? What would they think of me spending my time at home all day doing nothing but sitting in front of the computer and typing? Would they bug my phone, examine my hard drive, read my email, watch the sites I surfed? What would they make of my choice in sites? Should I not have looked at that particular news story?

Thankfully the paranoia was not quite a constant companion, but periodically it would peek out from its hiding place and wink at me; I tried to chase it away with reason. Especially when I noticed a car parked outside our house and I peered at the two old people sitting there and worried what they might be up to—until another pair of old people appeared walking up my driveway carrying copies of the *Watchtower*.

And then on another ordinary day in March, after two years, it simply came to an end.

My phone rang. I picked it up, and my attorney informed me that the lawsuit against us had been dismissed. It was over. I thanked him profusely, and felt an enormous burden fall off my back, a burden larger than I had fully comprehended. When I hung up, I found myself crying, weeping uncontrollably; I called and told Ruth, and called other people to let them know, having a hard time holding back the tears.  I found myself crying unexpectedly at odd moments, like singing a hymn the next Sunday morning at church.

And of course, all troubles did not end.

That very night, when Ruth and I went out to celebrate, on our way home, our van stopped working: the transmission died and we were suddenly faced with a one thousand, eight-hundred-dollar bill for fixing that—which was money we didn't have.  But it was easy, after having a thirty-one million dollar lawsuit dismissed, to keep one thousand eight-hundred dollars in perspective and to think to myself, "you know, if God took care of a thirty-one million dollar problem, perhaps, just perhaps, he can take care of a one thousand eight-hundred dollar problem." Which he did.  But that has been one of the few times in my life when I was able to keep my perspective and not lose it and start wailing like Jacob that "everything is against me."

## Chapter Three: The Reason for the Question

How often do we hear platitudes: the sweet words that pretend to comfort us. Clichés along the following lines:

- God will never give you more than you can handle.
- God wants you to be healthy and wealthy.
- If you only read the Bible more, pray more and get all the sin out of your life, then God will be able to pour out his blessings upon you.
- If you are not living the life you want to have, then you need to find out what you're doing that is standing in the way of God's blessing.

Have we not heard that sort of stuff on a regular basis? Do we not, in our heart of hearts, believe that there must be some secret, some missing piece to a puzzle, some key to a fulfilled life where all will be as I would like it to be?

And do we not, at the same time, harbor the thought, perhaps fearfully, that all those platitudes are bunk? We're not wrong to doubt it all.

Because our hidden thought, our secret fear, is the truth! Those platitudes are fantasy. They are wishful thinking. They have nothing to do with the world as it is.

Reality opposes our fantasies, our hopes, our desires. It blocks what we really want.

Why is that?

We believe that we are doing something wrong and that's why our lives are less than perfect. We want to believe that wrong actions on our part, wrong beliefs, wrong thoughts, wrong *something,* is responsible for our suffering.

Because then we could fix everything.  The power would belong to us.

There is the world that we wish for and then there is the world that is. We would do well to learn to live in the world that is, rather than the ideal we wish could be.  The worldview of too many, the worldview reflected in the clichés that begin this chapter, strike me as beautiful sentiments that fit reality as well as the hobo song, *Big Rock Candy Mountain*:

> *On a summer day in the month of May a burly*
> *bum came hiking*
> *Down a shady lane through the sugar cane, he*
> *was looking for his liking.*
> *As he roamed along he sang a song of the land of*
> *milk and honey*
> *Where a bum can stay for many a day, and he*
> *won't need any money...*

As we have become more prosperous in the modern world, we have allowed ourselves to start believing in a false god, the god of the clichés, the god of Big Rock Candy Mountain.

But that god does not exist.

Atheists rightly reject the god that permeates so much of the blatherings of televangelists, and in a less strong form (there is a strong and weak form of the Big Rock Candy god) it appears in popular entertainment and for that matter, even in far too many ordinary churches.  But the Big Rock Candy god is not real.  And thus the atheists are right to reject him, just as Christianity in its early days was atheistic in regard to Zeus and Thor.

It is time for Christianity to regain its ancient atheism and like the common modern atheist, to reject this false god as it has done all the other pretenders before it.  The Church needs to embrace the actual God—the real God—the one we see in the Bible and in the world around us, instead of the make-believe Big Rock Candy one that so many inexplicably find comfort in.

There is so much I don't understand.  I do not understand a mother deserting her husband and children for another relationship in another state.  I do not understand why she abandoned all her friends, people she had known and cared about for years, people that genuinely cared for her—without so much as a goodbye or explanation.  The loss of that friend is just a tiny hole in my life, compared to the giant gap in the lives of a husband who now works seven days a week to try to make ends meet while he raises his children by himself, children who must try to understand how their mother must no longer love them.

I do not understand the death of a friend's daughter, a young woman barely past her teens, from an accidental overdose of prescription drugs.

I do not understand the death of another friend's only son in a car accident in which he was the passenger, leaving behind his young wife and three-year-old daughter. How does this new widow explain to her daughter that daddy really isn't going to come home again, despite her tiny certainty that, "of course he'll be home, mommy."

I do not understand why a young man decided to take his own life, leaving behind grieving friends, parents, and siblings, along with questions that can never be answered.

The never-ending tragedies tear at the fabric of my soul.  They are like tiny moths, eating away at it, leaving it filled with holes from which drips nothing but pain and puzzlement.  These serious traumas cause doubt and pain and force considered thought. But rather than the larger pains, it is the small tragedies of life that torment us most frequently, most incessantly: the hurts in those close to us, the pain of the day-to-day grind, of the flat tires and the bounced checks and the unpaid bills; the suffering of the children talking back, not making the team, scraping by with C's, listening to music I don't like and hanging with friends that make me worry; coming home late and not being good about calling.

Worst of all, however, are the disasters of cosmic proportion that rip the fabric to shreds.

September 11, 2001. Terrorists hijacked four passenger jetliners. They crashed two of them into the World Trade Center, destroying the buildings and killing close to three thousand people. Meanwhile, another of the planes crashed into the Pentagon, killing over two hundred people there, and the final aircraft crashed into a field in Pennsylvania killing all on board after its passengers heroically fought back, preventing that plane from reaching its intended target, likely either the U.S. Capitol building or the White House.

Days like 911 raise questions in all our minds regarding the nature of existence, about the goodness of God, about what it really is that God wants and expects out of all of us. It makes us wonder if God's existence is even compatible with the world full of pain in which we endure until our own inevitable deaths.

How do we live in a world where horrors can happen? How do we face the crises of life, both small and great? Is there some key to life, some playbook we can get, some list we can follow, some formula we can memorize that will get us through this world in one piece, with ourselves and our families living long, productive and prosperous lives?

If God is good, if he loves us, and if he's all powerful, then why do bad things happen to good people? Or, more to the point: why do bad things happen to me? As frequently as we hear this question asked, as frequently as we ourselves muse about it, we likely imagine it to be the sort of question human beings have always asked themselves: that it is an ancient question.

This is not quite the case, however.

In fact, the question of why suffering happens is actually a modern one.

The book of Job in the Bible and the other examples of wisdom literature that stand beside it in the corpus of scripture, along with similar literary examples from the Ancient Near East and elsewhere are trotted out as proof that the question is as old as the human race and as universal.

But yet, in reality, if we read through the ancient literatures without imposing the modern way of looking at things upon it, we do not find any of the ancients actually ever asking the question as we express it.  Job never once asks, "can there be a God when the world is, as a modern president might put it, a 'sh**hole'?"

Likewise, no other ancient culture ever asked that, either.  We have to wait until the likes of Voltaire in eighteenth century France, or Leibniz in eighteenth century Germany, to find the specific question—and the two inevitable responses to the question: Leibniz answering "yes," the existence of God can be reconciled with the question of suffering, and Voltaire's loud "no" in *Candide*.

Many argue that there is no real answer to the question. Others say that the question proves there is no God.  Others say that the answer has something to do with free will.

In 1979 Douglas Adams published his bestselling book, *The Hitchhiker's Guide to the Galaxy*.  In it, he told the story of a group of hyper-intelligent pan-dimensional beings who demand to learn the "Ultimate Answer to the Ultimate Question of Life, The Universe, and Everything" from the supercomputer, Deep Thought, which was specially built for this purpose. It takes Deep Thought seven and a half million years to compute and check the answer, which turns out to be 42. Unfortunately, according to Deep Thought, the problem is that "The Ultimate Question" is itself unknown.

When asked to produce "The Ultimate Question," the computer says that it cannot; however, it can help to design an even more powerful computer—the Earth—that can. The programmers then embark on a further ten-million-year program to discover The Ultimate Question.

The answer to the question that so bothers so many—how could a good God let me suffer like this—*is* 42.

How so?  None of the proposed solutions or answers satisfies fully, or even seems to make all that much sense. They all seem as nonsensical as the answer proposed in Douglas Adams' novel.  A non-sequitur. No answer at all.

The proposed solutions to suffering fall into the following categories:

**"Something to do with free will."**  The movie *Time Bandits* offers up this answer toward the end of the film, when the bandits come upon the Creator, and ask him about the horrors of the world.  He offers up that single line, almost as an afterthought, which hardly satisfies anyone. Platinga, the theologian and philosopher, offers up much the same answer which he calls "free will theism."

**"The Best of All Possible Worlds."** Leibnitz offers this as his solution, which is really no solution but merely an affirmation or a foot stomp.  His argument is that, given that God is good, all powerful, and all knowing, then the universe he created—our universe—must by definition then be the best of all possible worlds, since, if a better world were possible, then God, given who and what he is, would have created that one instead.  Since we live in this world, this must be the best one that is possible—and then he adds the same caveat as Platinga (among others)—given human free will.  Voltaire's critique, which appears in his short novel *Candide,* argues that if this is as good as it gets, then maybe we should consider the possibility that a better solution to the issue of suffering is then just to assume there is no creator in the first place, or at least if there is one, to assume he just doesn't care.  Others have suggested that perhaps God isn't good, or that he isn't all powerful, or that he isn't all knowing—or some combination of all of those. Hans Kung, among other theologians in what is known as process theology, have argued in this direction.

**"There is no God."** Atheism, of the modern sort since Voltaire at least, argues that the obvious answer to the question of suffering is that there is no god of any sort, certainly not the sort of deities proposed in any faith tradition ranging from ancient paganism to the more recent monotheisms. Of course, the obvious objection, such as it is, to atheism is that it ends up as a rather bleak outlook—many human beings find it too sad, too despairing. And beyond that, it still fails to fully solve or address the problem of suffering or evil.

How so?

Well, with atheism we are now *alone* in the face of our suffering. Suffering and evil still exist: that problem has not gone away. But at least now there is no one out there who even pretends to care.

So yeah, I feel so much better. Not. This "solution" is just *so* bleak.

Of course, atheists would wisely respond that how reality makes us feel is really neither here nor there. Most people don't get warm fuzzies about any of the laws of physics, after all, but reality is what it is, and, from an atheist perspective, well, reality just bites. Get used to disappointment.

And, so, each of these answers, when the fat is trimmed away, are just the answer that Deep Thought gave: 42.

* * *

That's why no one is ever satisfied by the answer anyone gives to the "ultimate question."

How so?

Because the reality of the whole debate is fundamentally like that of Douglas' Adam's story: no one

48

is asking the right question. *It is the question itself that is nonsense.* Thus, all the answers that people make up are as meaningful as the one that Douglas Adams proposed in his humorous novel. You can't get an answer that makes sense if the question is garbage.

The answer, the reality of God and the reality of suffering and reconciling those two things is really not so difficult. It took the modern world to come up with the wrong question—a question that seemed like such a good one at the time it was asked that it has since become hard to see that it is ridiculously bad and not the right question at all. It has mucked things up so badly that everyone is now so thoroughly confused they can't see the obvious.

The story is told of the physicist Wolfgang Pauli, that one day a friend of his showed Pauli the paper of a young physicist which he suspected was not of much value. Pauli looked over the paper and then commented, "It is not even wrong." The idea being, that the paper was based on such invalid reasoning and speculative premises that it was hard to figure out how to even begin countering it: there was just so much that would have to be unpacked first.

The ancients were undisturbed by the issue of suffering that has so flummoxed us today, because it is a non-issue. And it's not that the ancients were somehow stupid and couldn't see what to us seems so obvious. Instead, they just hadn't considered asking such a stupid, nonsensical question. It's akin to a chess master being confounded by a novice chess player—not because the novice is somehow brilliant but because the novice made a move so boneheaded that it blindsided the master expecting a competent move. Or, one might say that the modern question regarding suffering is akin to asking what happens when an irresistible force comes up against an immovable object. It sounds profound, until you point out that by definition, the question is nonsense: if an object is immovable, by definition there is not a force that can jar it;

if a force is irresistible, there is no object that can stand against it.

Once we ask the *right* question, the answer becomes obvious.  42 is a perfectly satisfactory answer if you ask the right question: the question that goes with the real answer.

## Chapter Four: Complaints

We all have complaints. The length of time the local hamburger place took to get around to giving me my meal gave a whole new meaning to the term "fast" food. I hadn't intended to fast, and what's worse, I violated what Jesus said about not letting on that I was doing it: I complained. I've complained about the cable going off for no reason. I complained about the time my phone was shut off when I mistakenly *over*paid my phone bill.

Doubtless Jacob, the patriarch in the Bible, complained more than a few times during the course of a very long life. But there was once, when he was an old man, that the Bible records he made the following complaint: "everything is against me."

On the face of it, he had good reason to gripe. Better reason than I have to complain about waiting ten minutes for my fast food burger. Life threw Jacob some lemons, and when he tried to make lemonade, he found out he was out of sugar and the lemons were rotten. Of course, Jacob's perspective was off just a tad, too. It is, after all, hard to keep one's perspective in the middle of a tornado. But reality hasn't changed just because we happen to be a little dizzy at the moment.

How do we live in a world where things go wrong? How do we face the crises of life, both small and great? Is there some key to life, some playbook we can get, some list we can follow, some formula we can memorize that will get us through this world in one piece, with ourselves and our families living long, productive and prosperous lives?

### The Search for Answers

Prosperity, peace, health, love and acceptance, happiness: these are the desires of our hearts.  We spend hours and lots of money in their pursuit.  We find ourselves buying the latest gadget, going to the hottest movie, buying certain foods and cars, almost as if we believe that what is missing in our lives can be satisfied by stuffing more things into them.  And of course, we know, if we ever slow down a bit and think about it, that the hole inside will not be filled by either a Hummer or that new plasma screen television.

And it is not something that only those outside the church do.  In the church, we find ourselves frustrated, convinced that there must be something that we're missing still.  We are not achieving the fullness of the life that we know God wants us to have.  Where is the peace we were promised, the abundant living we thought we were guaranteed?

Why are my children talking back to me, why am I not completely enamored of my spouse?  Why do I have trouble making ends meet, why do I feel so tired and stressed?  Why do I still worry and feel frustrated?  Why do I still feel tempted to look at those pictures on the web, or eat too much cake, or wonder, sometimes, if maybe I would be happier living somewhere else, or being with someone else, or going to a different church, or finding a different pastor, or reading this book, or seeing that video, or going to that conference or seminar?

Maybe I'm not praying right.  Maybe I need to get the sin out of my life.  Maybe I need to read my Bible more.  What am I missing?  What key do I need to unlock the blessings of God and finally achieve the wonderful life I know God wants me to have?

Or is it all a lie?

Maybe God really wants me to be unhappy?  Or have I screwed up so badly now that I'm beyond hope?  Have I committed the unpardonable sin?  Has God set me on the shelf?  Will he no longer use me?  Will I now just mark time, and have to eat straw for the rest of my miserable, worthless existence?

### Jacob's Struggle

Jacob's life was not an easy one and his family life, both growing up, and then as an adult would fit the modern definition of "dysfunctional."  He and his mother had conspired together to defraud both his father and his fraternal twin brother.  When he had to leave home out of fear that his swindled brother might actually kill him, he went to live with Laban, his mother's brother.

Laban was a crafty fellow, and noticed that Jacob had quickly taken a shine to his younger daughter.  So, Laban consented to a marriage between them, on the condition that Jacob work for him as a virtual slave for seven years first.  Only at the end of that time could he then wed Rachel.

So, the blessed day finally arrived.  The Bible tells us that the seven years had seemed but a few days because of Jacob's love for Rachel.  Jacob survived the wedding ceremony, then partied like there was no tomorrow—and when tomorrow came, he found himself in bed with Rachel's older sister.

Laban had tricked Jacob. During the festivities, old Laban had switched daughters.  "Oh," he explained, "it's an old custom around here that the older daughter must always marry first.  But seeing as how you're family now, I'll work a good deal for you.  You wanted Rachel?  No problem.  Here, just sign on for another seven year stint with me and you can have her—and just because I like you so much, you can marry her right after you finish the honeymoon time with my older daughter. Her name's Leah by the way.  Remember?"

As if that wasn't a big enough problem, once he did marry Rachel, she had trouble getting pregnant. But her sister, Leah, was having no such difficulty.  So Rachel was miserable.  Following the customs of the day, Jacob agreed to take her maidservant as a third wife, so that she could serve as a surrogate to bear children for Rachel.  And then, almost at once, Leah became infertile too, so by the time all is said and done, Jacob wound up with a fourth wife to do the same for Leah as he was doing for Rachel.

In the course of time, however, Rachel did get pregnant.  She gave birth to a son, whom she named Joseph.  Some while later, she was expecting again.  But it was a hard pregnancy and given the lack of modern medical technology, she died in childbirth.  The son survived, however, and Jacob named him Benjamin.

Jacob showed obvious favoritism to Joseph, the first-born son of the one woman out of the four that he had actually loved.  This did not endear Joseph to his other, by that time, ten brothers.  The fraternal resentment grew to such an extreme that the ten brothers determined to murder Joseph.  But at the last minute, rather than kill him, they realized they could be rid of him and make some money at the same time.  They sold Joseph to a passing group of traders.  Then they took the fancy clothes that Jacob had given Joseph, roughed them up a bit and dipped them in goat blood.  They told their elderly father, "look what we found, do you suppose this means that poor Joseph has been torn to pieces by a lion or something?"

Jacob was heartbroken, and the brothers were secretly pleased. No more Joseph. Easy money. Life was good.

The story continues: the traders sold Joseph into slavery in Egypt, where, through a course of events that would distract our story here, he winds up rising to favor with the Pharaoh—the king—of Egypt and becomes his second in command.

Meanwhile, famine came to the world, both in Egypt and in Palestine, where Jacob was living.  Thanks to Joseph, Egypt was continuing to prosper and had food in abundance—but for a price.  So Jacob sent his ten oldest sons down to Egypt with money and told them to buy provision so that they wouldn't starve to death.

When they got there, Joseph recognized them right off, though of course his brothers didn't.  It's been twenty-five years and they *know* they sold Joseph as a slave and so chances are he's dead by now anyhow; perhaps they've almost convinced themselves the story they told their old man was the truth.  In any case, Joseph torments them for awhile, then arrests one of the brothers, Simeon, and locks him in jail.  He tells the remaining nine brothers that if they ever hope to see Simeon again, then the next time they come to Egypt they'd best bring Benjamin, their youngest brother with them.  Or else.  And so away the nine remaining brothers go.

When they arrived back home, they told Jacob their tale of woe about Simeon, about how harshly they were treated, and about the demand for Benjamin to meet the Egyptian governor.  As if that weren't bad enough, there seemed to have been a mix-up in the whole transaction, because though they did at least return with the food they'd been sent to get, the Egyptian authorities had apparently been shortchanged: the money they had given to pay for it all was somehow still in their bags.  So now the Egyptians would be sending the bill collectors out to get them if they didn't get that taken care of soon.

To say the least, Jacob was not at all happy.  The one true love of his life was dead.  Joseph, his favorite, the oldest son of his beloved, had been dead for twenty-five years.  And now Simeon had been taken from him, and that monster in Egypt was demanding the last link he had to his beloved!  Beside himself with grief, we can read his reaction in Genesis 42:36 where it all comes down to this:

Their father Jacob said to them, "You have deprived me of my children. Joseph is no more and Simeon is no more, and now you want to take Benjamin. Everything is against me!"

And certainly it was the case that the circumstances of his life were unbearably bad. From his perspective, from the perspective of his sons standing around him, his complaint was fully reasonable, perfectly understandable, and self-evidently true.

And yet, the fascinating thing about his words is that we know that he couldn't be more wrong! This, despite the fact that his words seemed so obviously true to Jacob—unassailably true, in fact. But we the readers of this episode know some things that Jacob didn't know. In fact, we know facts that Jacob *couldn't* know. *We* know that Joseph was not only not dead, but he was second in command in Egypt, the most powerful and most wealthy nation on the planet at that time.

The reality of Jacob's existence is that everything could hardly be better. His favorite son has done very well for himself, thank you. Good job, and great future, with money to burn. *Poor Jacob simply doesn't know this yet.* His perception, his *perspective* of reality, is incorrect.

We, the readers, can do nothing to alleviate Jacob's suffering. God didn't do anything about it either. It'll be another year before Jacob learns the truth of what his life is *really* like, in contrast to his perception of it. For twenty-five years he mourned for someone who was not dead. He bemoans his fate as a miserable one, though his family is powerful and prosperous.

### The Quest for the Abundant Life

A lot of Christians are running around looking for the way to fix all the problems in their lives, convinced that if they could only learn the secret, discover the magic words, find the special knowledge, locate the missing puzzle pieces, then suddenly life would be okay: their kids will behave and do well in school, they'll be able to pay all their bills on time and they'll get out of debt; they will find that their wives or husbands are now gorgeous.  Their cars will stop breaking down and never be more than three years old, their sleep will be sweet, and their health problems will be a thing of the past.  They will eat whatever they want and never grow fat, and exercise will be a pleasure.  Not only that, but they will suddenly have a theologian's understanding of God and the Bible and so all will be well.

They see people out there who live like that, or seem to live like that, and so they try to fathom what secret recipe they followed, what prayers they offered, that got God to grant them this wonderful, abundant life.  And of course, that's what all people wish for: a life free from pain, a life of abundance, a life of blessing.  And surely, *surely* the reason I don't have that life right now is because I've missed something, done something wrong, followed a wrong path, made a wrong choice.  But if I read the right books, see the right pastor, listen to the right tapes, follow the right program, view the right video series, then that'll take care of it.  The thing that has been hidden from me will finally be in the open.

Millions of Christians drop enormous amounts of money and time going from place to place hoping to find the abundant life.  For a while, things look pretty good after a seminar or after finishing a book.  After all, the seminar or book promises that if the advice is followed then happiness will surely follow; the secret is finally secured.  All I have to do now is follow these steps and do these easy things.  So the happy Christian carefully follows the items on the list, and a few days go by or a few weeks, and he or she changes her life, and throws out the things that the book says would hinder the coming of the abundant life, and she adds the things that will bring it: a regimen begins, a checking off of boxes, of prayers said, Bible passages read and memorized, ideas gotten into the skull.  Thus, the days pass, the weeks, and sometimes the months or even a few years.

But, despite all that effort, all that activity, all that following of the rules—life remains more or less the same. The car needs tires, and the check book is empty. The boy decides he wants an earring and you look in the mirror and you have some more wrinkles and the hair isn't quite as shiny as it used to be and the color seems to be fading and then the doctor tells you that you need to lose weight, and the pain in your knee won't go away, and you get the flu.

Then you hear about another preacher come to town, and he tells you that all that stuff you did was good—real good—but look here, did you see *this*? And since you missed *that* then why would you wonder why your life is so messed up, why you're under your circumstances and not rising above them, and why your prayers go unanswered, and you haven't seen revival and no one got baptized in your little church, which, shame be told, is struggling each month to scrape together enough cash to pay the light bill, let alone the mortgage and the pastor.

And see *there*. If you weren't in debt, if you hadn't gone and disobeyed God on that point, then your life wouldn't be the shambles that it is. But see *here*, just buy these videos and this guidebook—and by the way, I can take Visa or Master Card—and you'll get your finances in order in no time. It's just a matter of following these simple steps. *See*?

The abundant life remains forever just over the next hill—if you are ever honest with yourself as you bop from place to place, person to person, looking for the thing that'll fill the hole in your life. *Tomorrow*, I'll see the light. So you struggle, and you follow the rules and you try to put on the face, and you know if you can only get good enough, and do just the right things, and that if there's no unconfessed sin in your life (and how, pray tell, do you keep up on *that*? "Father forgive me, for I have sinned; it has been five minutes since my last confession. I lusted twice, and I felt anger at that doofus who cut me off just now and…"). Maybe if you don't let the devil into your house, why *then*…everything will be fine.

Yet, late at night, when you stare at the ceiling, you know that lust in your heart, and your anger at wayward drivers, and the stack of past due notices, and that mysterious ache in your back, and that stranger in bed next to you that doesn't at all resemble the lover of your sweaty dreams, is still going to be there in the morning. And inside, you feel like a rat in a maze, pushing levers and getting pellets and wondering: if this is all there is, then why am I not happy, why do I not see satisfaction, where is the abundance I've been promised?

Does God not want me to be happy? Am I just supposed to learn to live with this, put up with it—stiff upper lip now, and all of that? If so, then I don't know if I want to go on living, I don't know if all the running about, all the work, all the lists and rules and the search for the holy grail is even worth the effort, since I really don't seem to be seeing any benefit from it. If I'm unhappy being good, then maybe it's time I try a little bad. Or put it another way, what's the point of the rules if life still sucks?

## Chapter Five: Part of the Question

Another one of the answers traditionally given for why bad things happen to good people is that "there is none righteous, no not one." Bad things happen to you because you're a sinner. You deserve to suffer. This is an inadequate—and false guilt inducing response to the question of why do the righteous suffer: it "eliminates" the problem by simply claiming that one of the premises of the question is false, namely, the idea that there are any righteous.

There are theological holes aplenty in this simplistic—and wrongheaded—"solution." In Christ, we are declared righteous. Our righteousness is in Christ. And we are saved—made righteous—by Jesus' sacrifice, not by our actions whether good or bad or indifferent. Sure, in ourselves, apart from Jesus, we are not "righteous." But we are not apart from Jesus. Our righteousness is in Him and we are indeed righteous. The critique, the explanation, that there are no righteous and thus that the righteous therefore do not suffer, is simply bogus.

This was how Job's friends responded to the suffering of Job. They spent the bulk of the book accusing Job of various evils and demanding that he confess. Their fear, throughout, was that Job was telling the truth when he said he'd done nothing amiss. And they were furious with what he told them, that bad things happen to both the good and the bad, without discrimination: pain and suffering are equal opportunity employers. You can do everything right and suffer horribly, or be a scumbag and be rich, famous, and trouble free for a long, prosperous and happy life. Job's friends' response to this information from Job was to tell him that his point of view would undermine piety. After all, why be good if you don't get anything for it?

Why work hard if you're still going to be poor?  Why make good choices if you're still going to get kicked in the teeth?

That's the question Satan had asked God at the very beginning of the story: "Does Job serve God for nothing?" Job's problems came to him precisely to answer that question: why does Job serve God?  Is it really because God gave him good stuff?  What if God was mean to him? Would Job still remain faithful?

Of course, that's the uncomfortable question, the elephant in the room as it were, for all of us.  Why is it that we are good?  Why is it that we serve God?  What is it we want to get out of it?  And of course, then the questions become more complex.  Can I really be good at all if I'm just doing it for reward?  That's not really altruistic; how righteous is that, then?  Is anyone at all righteous?

And doesn't God reward or curse people?  Don't we have examples in the Bible of bad things happening to bad people?  Haven't we seen it in real life?  Isn't our whole justice system based on the concept of punishment?  Don't we get good grades in school when we do good work, and poor marks if we don't?  Are there not winners and losers on the field of play, in war, in business?  We get paid and keep our jobs if we are good at them, sometimes we get awards, and don't we get fired if we screw up?  So shouldn't we then answer the question of "why do the righteous suffer?" by saying that, well, if they're suffering, they aren't really righteous?  They deserve it.  The four-year-old dying of brain cancer: she deserves it, or her parents do.  Same for the baby that dies of SIDS, or the miscarriage.  Those people starving in Haiti?  They're a bunch of non-Christian voodoo sinners, so God's getting them.  Same for those people who died in the tsunami, or that earthquake, or from the plague.  Those babies starving: they're all sinners: "born in sin, sinful since my mother conceived me."  And so on.

Satisfying?  Clear?

"How's that working for you?" to paraphrase Dr. Phil.

I don't think this is a solution at all.  It is *completely* wrongheaded.

This of course leads to what we see all too much of: piling on those who are suffering.  It is not bad enough that they are grieving some tragedy, now we need to make them feel guilty, too. We can even quote the Bible to drive the guilt home (context and nuance be damned, of course). These are some of the favorites of those who would add a heaping helping of guilt on top of people suffering:

> But when he asks, he must believe and not doubt, because he who doubts is like a wave of the sea, blown and tossed by the wind. That man should not think he will receive anything from the Lord; he is a double-minded man, unstable in all he does. (James 1:6-8)

And

> You want something but don't get it. You kill and covet, but you cannot have what you want. You quarrel and fight. You do not have, because you do not ask God. When you ask, you do not receive, because you ask with wrong motives, that you may spend what you get on your pleasures. (James 4:2-3)

So if we spring off these passages from James' letter, these are the reasons you are suffering, according to those who believe all suffering is somehow related to justified guilt:

• You suffer, you lack, because you don't have faith.  Or not enough of it.

• So you lack what you need because you're a sinner.  You haven't confessed all those sins or repented of them.  Maybe there's one or more you forgot about and until you remember and list them off, God can't bless you.

•   Or you have doubt, not enough faith. So maybe if you'd just pray harder, squinch up your face a bit more, or maybe start fasting, perhaps, then God could finally rescue you.

•   Or maybe you aren't really wanting God's will for your life?  Maybe you're resisting God's will and this suffering you're experiencing, such as seeing your baby die of cancer, is really what's best for you.  Instead of moaning about the death of your loved one you should be dancing in the streets; this death is really a blessing (if you squinch up your face, squint, and look at it cross-eyed).

•   Or, just maybe, you want to consume it all on your lusts. You're just being unbearably selfish in not wanting your child to suffer. You are asking for the wrong thing, to misuse your child's health, and that's why you're suffering. Sinner that you are.

In some sense, according to Christianity, it is the case that there are no righteous people. Paul in the beginning of his letter to the Christians in Rome stresses that all human beings, regardless of their behavior, are evil.  He makes it unequivocal:

> "There is no one righteous, not even one;
> there is no one who understands;
> there is no one who seeks God.
> All have turned away,
> they have together become worthless;
> there is no one who does good,
> not even one." (Romans 3:10-12)

Kant argues similarly, that there are no wholly altruistic actions. We do what we do, ultimately, because it benefits us in some way: nothing is unselfish.  This was used to humorous effect in the *Friends* episode, "The One

Where Phoebe Hates PBS." Phoebe repeatedly attempts and fails to find a selfless good deed despite repeated attempts.

Because all are under the wrath of God, only God had the ability to fix our problem. The death of God—of Jesus—solved it and it is applied to people not according to their ability to do or not do good, but by grace. God grants mercy and forgiveness for free, removing behavior from the mix altogether. The more recent television series, *The Good Place* ends the first season in a similar place in that the "mistake" that "Fake Elinore" is in the Good Place is revealed to not be an error at all due to the fact that it isn't really the Good Place after all, but is in fact the Bad Place. The characters discover the awful news that all of them are condemned, and all of them are in the Bad Place. Worse, the best people, the good people, the people who seem to be the most righteous, are revealed to be "not good" due to their lack of selflessness in their "doing good."

Why does this matter?  Why is something not really good due to it not being "selfless"?

Consider:

1.   Fairness.  The circumstances of life—good or bad: if you grew up oppressed, mistreated and poor or if you grew up dominant, wealthy and privileged.  How much better might your behavior be in a privileged position than not?  A poor person might, in the face of hunger, steal, or get involved in drug dealing in order to make ends meet. Or if a person is abused, might they be more likely to become an abuser themselves?  If they had poor parenting, never were taught good morals or given a work ethic, how much worse might their lives be as opposed to a person who grew up in a comfortable environment, with loving parents, who saw to their care, moral training and the like? What if you have a serious mental illness that makes it hard for you to even think clearly or comprehend reality?

Circumstances beyond the individual's ability to control have an enormous role in steering behavior.

2.     Satan's question to God about Job comes into play all the time.  Of course Job is good, Satan argues, since God blessed and protected him.  If that protection is removed, Satan wonders, if Job's life goes to pot—then what is likely to happen?  Perhaps sometimes such a Job will continue on the path of righteousness.   But realistically, how likely is that?  Is Job the exception or the rule?

3.     Consider a rich man.  Are his "friends" friendly because they genuinely like him, or because he is rich?  For that matter, don't people love us, like us, put up with us only because we provide some benefit to them or fill some need in their lives?  We are nice, perhaps, or helpful—we don't punch them in the nose.  If we always irritated a person, or hurt them in some way, would they remain our friends?  Probably about as long as a rich man's friends would hang with him if he suddenly lost everything and became impoverished.

So, can *any* behavior be truly good if it is not selfless?

What is good, then?  Is anything or anyone?

4.  Selfishness, by its very nature, is considered wrong.  How often were we told while growing up, "don't be selfish"?   Selfishness is the motivation for gluttony.  Gluttony is not being overweight; gluttony is not eating too much.  That's a modern misunderstanding of the sin.  In reality, gluttony is taking more than my fair share.  Gluttony is satisfying myself at the expense of others.  Gluttony is eating my food and the food of my neighbor.  Gluttony is caring only for myself.   And that is the problem: being good, doing the right thing: it is never pure.  *Always*, there is the part of it that is all about me: what I will get from it, the benefit that will accrue to me.  For I, if nothing else, feel good, better, to have done right than wrong.  I get a tax deduction for my act of charity, my

name appears on a plaque for my gift. I receive positive notoriety for my generosity. Even if anonymous, I know that I did it and I feel a warm fuzzy. My right hand knows very well what my left hand is doing.

### The Imposed Righteousness of Believers

Of course, all this criticism of the possibility of anyone being righteous fails to reckon with the obvious: as Christians, we have been declared righteous. By God. We are saved not by what we do but by what Jesus did. So, behavior has been eliminated from the equation altogether. Our righteousness is in Christ. When God looks at us, he sees Jesus, who already took the rap for our bad deeds. All our debts have been paid. Our credit is stellar. We are perfect.

### The Devil's Advocate Responds

The atheists and skeptics, of course, have a simple solution for all of this concern with good people suffering. For them, suffering proves that God doesn't exist. If God were good and loving, he'd make you happy, he'd alleviate your suffering. Especially if he thinks you're righteous. There is no explanation for this poor treatment, this miserable nature of your existence, and so that means only one possible conclusion: there simply is no God. You suffer because the universe is random and capricious. The odds are just not in your favor. Too bad.

Is this quick and dirty solution to the question of suffering justified? It is the answer proposed by Voltaire in his response to Leibnitz's *Theodicy* in which Leibnitz argued "this is the best of all possible worlds." Voltaire reacted with his short novel *Candide*, when he demonstrated, at least to his own satisfaction, that Leibnitz's proposal was absurd. In *Candide*, Voltaire seeks to demonstrate that this world is an awful place, not at all the "best of all possible worlds" that Leibniz was arguing for.  Of course, there is a problem with Voltaire's response: it is a strawman argument.  Leibniz never argued that this was the "best of all possible worlds" which would suggest Leibniz believed the world was perfect.  Instead, Leibniz argued that this was the best of all possible worlds given the caveat of human free will.  That is, the full concept that Leibniz was arguing was that, given sentient creatures that have the ability to make mostly unconstrained choices, this is as good as it gets.

**So, God is Unnecessary?**
The Bible asks, "who is God?" and "what does he want?"

The Bible never asks, "is he real?"

Even so, those who argue that God does not exist will point out that the burden of proof must rest with those who say he does.  After all, those who insist on the reality of the Loch Ness monster are required to offer irrefutable evidence.  It is not up to the rest of us to demonstrate that they are mistaken.  As Carl Sagan famously said, "extraordinary claims require extraordinary proof."  Skeptics therefore argue that those who believe in God carry the burden of making the case for Him.

Given that a belief in the existence of the divine, however conceived, has been a part of the human race since its beginning, and since the existence of the divine was not questioned until relatively recently, I'm not entirely certain that the burden of proof indeed rests with those who believe in God or gods.  That is, the assumption by skeptics is that the existence of God is an extraordinary claim, like claiming elves exist.  Is that actually the case?  Or is it the other way around: is claiming there is no God the more extraordinary claim?  Why the assumption—and it is an assumption—that God's existence is extraordinary, and his non-existence is ordinary and the proper default position?

Or put it this way: what burden exists upon those who claim for a new idea or explanation?  Just because the skeptics *say* it belongs to the believers in the divine, does not mean that they are actually right in foisting it upon them.  But my question goes even further than that.

I wonder, in fact, whether there is any need for proof at all.

Skeptics will point out that there are logical explanations for the hows and whys of many things that happen in the universe, things that our ancestors attributed to God.  We do not believe any longer that lightning is being tossed down on us by an angry Zeus.  So is it reasonable to believe then, that those things which still beg of explanation thereby prove God must be responsible for them?  Isn't it more likely, in fact, that we will find explanations for the remaining mysteries?  In fact, why should it be necessary to invoke God at all?  Can't we say that God is, in all such cases, "unnecessary" as an explanation?

This conclusion should neither shock nor alarm those of us who continue to believe that God (however conceived) does, in fact, exist. I should add, however that demonstrating Zeus does not exist, or that the Pastafarian noodle deity is a joke, does not mean that an argument for any and every conceivable deity is likewise a joke or otherwise ludicrous.  Proving—or disproving—unicorns does not disprove or demonstrate in any way that either horses or zebras or antelope or goats do not exist.  Proving there are not intelligent aliens on Mars says nothing about their existence on some other well-positioned and apportioned planet elsewhere in the universe.  That Jennifer Aniston is not my wife does not mean that I do not have a beautiful wife.

**God's existence is not postulated as an explanation**

God's existence is not postulated as an *explanation* for anything by the biblical writers. His existence is simply assumed, and he is then described by his actions. It is a common mistake for theists to postulate God as an explanation for whatever might currently be inexplicable. It's akin to exclaiming after a near-disaster, or after an unexpectedly wonderful occurrence (as for instance receiving a free ice cream cone), "Now I know there's a God."

Um. No. You don't.

Although those who believe in God for many years have used God as the reason for why things happen: for why there is a universe, for how human beings come to be, or even, more recently, for how such things as eyes exist. Those who believe in God use that which people don't understand or can't explain as proof that there must be a God.

The Bible, however, never does this.

Perhaps that's an important clue.

Moreover, consider this pattern of behavior from the backside, from those who reject God: we who believe in God do not fully understand why the righteous suffer, why sin exists, or why God doesn't stop it. And yet, such ignorance of that which is sad is often used as proof by skeptics that there can be no God. They argue that if God existed, then surely there would be no suffering. The argument of skeptics is the same as the argument of believers. The difference is merely in the choice of the unknown: what is being displayed as inexplicable.

Is the skeptic's use of the inexplicable existence of pain and suffering of mortals in order to call into question the reality of God any more valid than a theist using the ignorance of how the universe began as proof that God *is*?

I don't think so. Consider an imperfect (as all must be) analogy:

I'm walking along one morning and slip.  I look at the floor and notice a pile of green goo.  I don't know why there is green goo on the floor.  I don't know where it came from.

So of course I immediately conclude that God must have made it, thereby proving his existence.

Say what?

The skeptic will wonder about how hard I must have banged my head on the floor.  My conclusion is nonsense, he avers.  If there was a God, then there would be no green goo at all, since the green goo is obviously bad.  A good and loving God would never allow green goo to exist.  Therefore, there must be no God.

Huh?

Are *either* of us making reasonable arguments?  Do either of us make sense?  Do either of our conclusions follow logically from our premises?

And yet.  When we theologians argue for the existence of God, or our opponents argue against him, we all use the same exact *form* of argument, just with slightly varied words—and everyone thinks we're being profound.

But I'm starting to think that we're in fact just being silly.

Let's look at some of the traditional arguments for God's existence and consider them in light of my green goo analogy.

### The Hoary Old Arguments for the Existence of God

Over the last thousand or more years, once persecution ended for the Christians of Europe and as Greek philosophy mixed with the thoughts of the church's theologians (who now had the leisure for thoughts since they no longer had to hide from Romans wanting to feed them to lions), said theologians began responding to less deadly threats to the faith and became concerned with a desire to prove that God—specifically the God of Christianity—existed.

Thomas Aquinas—in the thirteenth century (1225-1274 AD) listed several "proofs" for the existence of God. Specifically, he listed five: the unmoved mover, first cause, contingency, degree, and design (or teleological).

So what are the arguments? Let's begin with a quick summary of each of these five arguments that are given for the existence of God and then look at a couple of them in more detail.

The unmoved mover, also sometimes referred to as the prime mover, was proposed originally by Aristotle (or at least that's the first recorded instance we have). Aquinas developed the argument as follows: everything in the world around us that we see move does so because something sets it in motion; that is, things do not move on their own. Every movement has a cause. Thus, Aquinas called this original source of motion "the unmoved mover," or "the prime mover:" the thing that got everything else to start wandering about. This unmoved mover Aquinas then identified with God, specifically the Christian concept of God.

A related argument, growing from the idea of the unmoved mover, but separate from it, is listed second: the first cause argument. This is the idea that the universe, as a thing, like any other thing, must have had some cause. Rather than assume an infinite regression, Aquinas posits a first cause. That first cause is what we call God.

A third argument for the existence of God is called the contingency argument, or the necessary being argument. It works this way: all beings are contingent, that is, it is possible for them not to exist. Aquinas argues that if everything can possibly not exist, then there had to be a time when nothing existed. Since things do, in fact, now exist, there must exist a being whose existence is necessary. That being is what we call God.

Argument number four is labeled "degree." Aquinas argued that there are "degrees of goodness." That is, things are good as they are compared to other things and to a standard of goodness. This standard of goodness is then "maximum goodness" and it is the source and cause of all that can be called "good." This maximum goodness, this maximum good, is what we call God according to Aquinas.

Finally, the fifth argument for the existence of God is the design or teleological argument. It is an argument by analogy that points out that complex objects, such as clocks or watches or steam engines are crafted. Nintendo game systems do not just "happen." They are designed and built by designers and builders. The universe as a whole, living things in particular, are very complex; based on our experience with complex objects, Aquinas argues that the complexity of life, the universe and everything implies a great designer, a creator: the being we historically have called "God."

Most Christian apologetics begins with a discussion of these proofs. The two most commonly discussed of these proofs are First Cause and Design, primarily because those two seem to have the most going for them. That said, there remains a fundamental weakness for any of these traditional arguments for the existence of God.

It is a failure that is a general problem with Christian apologetics of any sort: Christians as they try to demonstrate the existence of God, wind up postulating God as the cause for anything inexplicable. On the surface, that might seem not unreasonable. But it really is a fundamental mistake. Arguing that God is the explanation for those things we can't explain is known as the "God-of-the-gaps" approach. That is, going back to the earlier story about the cat throw-up: we don't know where the green goo came from, so let's assume it came from God. That which is unknown or unexplained is God's doing. That is obviously nonsense in the case of the green goo, but it is equally nonsense no matter what we are attempting to explain.

The inevitable result, unsurprisingly, has been a growing irreconcilability between scientists and theologians. The position of many Christians has left them with a "God-who-is-spackle" who is constantly shrinking as scientific knowledge grows and shoves the divine spackle out of the way. The problem with "we don't understand this" so it must be God, is to ask the simple question. What happens when we *do* wind up understanding this? Does that mean God disappears?

Now, let's look at a couple of these traditional arguments for God in a bit more detail.

*First Cause*
One of Aquinas' arguments for the existence of God that we looked at is called "the first-cause argument." It goes something like this: every effect has a cause. The universe is an effect. Therefore the universe has a cause and that cause is God.

The problem with this argument is shown by asking a simple question: what is the cause of God? The Christian answer is that God is uncaused: he has always existed. Right away, the atheist can raise an objection: "Why must we assume that the universe has a cause? Perhaps the universe always existed." Additionally, one can raise the question: why should this imagined God be the God of the biblical stories? Why can't he be the god Zeus or the gods of the Babylonian creation epic? Why not the god imagined by deists? Or the Hindu pantheon?

Today, as a result of modern cosmology, a problem exists with the suggested objection that the world has always existed. All the scientific evidence points to the universe having a beginning: the Big Bang. This has been deeply disturbing to skeptics, because the question of causation now becomes very significant. In fact, the Big

Bang theory was only very slowly accepted by the scientific community precisely because of the uncomfortable theological implications of a beginning. And no explanation for the Big Bang has been found.

Yet.

Though there have, in the last few years, been some suggestions that might just work. That explanations for the Big Bang are being formulated by some researchers merely illustrates again the danger for Christians in the "God-of-the-gaps" or "God as spackle" approach. It is never wise to hop on an open question for which there is no firm answer and shout "Ah ha! God caused it. That proves God exists." Again, this is akin to arguing that the green goo, since we don't know where it came from, must come from God and thus proves God exists. I must repeat what I think is very obvious: arguments from ignorance are inherently weak.

If one ever takes a course in logic, one soon learns that one of the more common informal logical fallacies is called *"argumentum ad ignorantum"*: an argument from ignorance. That is, a lack of evidence by itself is no evidence at all.

Let's consider an example.

Joseph McCarthy is quoted as having once announced "There is nothing in the files to disprove his Communist connections." By itself, such a statement is nonsensical. A lack of evidence in such a case is simply no evidence at all. I have no evidence to indicate you don't beat your wife does not mean that you do, in fact, beat your wife. I haven't demonstrated any sort of guilt on your part.

Of course, sometimes it is reasonable to argue from a lack of evidence. For instance, in American criminal law, we presume that a defendant is innocent. The burden of proof is placed on the prosecution; if the prosecutor then fails to provide evidence of guilt, beyond a reasonable doubt, a jury must conclude that the defendant is not guilty. A lack of evidence in such a case does matter.

Likewise, if someone is making a new or what is generally thought to be an improbable claim, then the burden of proof is likewise on the person making the claim. So, if one were to claim that the President of the United States is a time traveler from the future, it is not an appeal to ignorance to point out that there is no evidence for such a proposition.

Also, it is not an appeal to ignorance in a closed system. The airport in Burbank, California has noise abatement regulations prohibiting flights in or out between midnight and 7 AM. Thus, if I then conclude there must be no arrivals from Panama City, Florida at 3 AM into the Burbank Airport because no such arrivals are listed, I have not made an appeal to ignorance, either. This is what is instead called a "closed world assumption."

There is another sort of reasoning that is not guilty of an appeal to ignorance. That is called "auto-epistemic" or "self-knowing." It involves reasoning from what one knows and what one would know if something were in fact true. So, for instance, it would be reasonable to say that at the age of sixty, if I had a superpower allowing me to see through walls, I would probably know it by now. Since I have never peered through walls, I don't have that superpower.

Likewise, if an extensive investigation has been undertaken, it may be reasonable to decide that something is in fact false based on a lack of any positive evidence for it. So, for instance, if after many years of study, no harmful effects have been demonstrated to occur from eating bananas, it is not unreasonable to assume that bananas are safe to consume.

I think it is safe to conclude, however, that if someone argues that since I don't have an explanation for where green goo comes from that it therefore comes from God is anything other than an appeal to ignorance. Likewise, my inability to explain the origin of green goo does not prove that God does not exist.  Either proposition is equally nonsensical and equally an appeal to ignorance.  On top of that, both are also non-sequiturs.

*Design*
The second of Aquinas' popular arguments for the existence of God is the teleological—that is, the argument from design. It is commonly formulated along these lines: if one finds a beautiful watch, one is legitimate in assuming a designer and builder for that watch. Are you, a human being, not a far more intricate machine than the finest watch? Isn't it reasonable to assume a designer for you?

The teleological argument is an argument by analogy, and by its nature, therefore, weak. A philosopher named Keith Lehrer in his book, *Philosophical Problems and Arguments: An Introduction*, states that such arguments can be summarized as follows:

• These three objects have these ten properties in common.

• Two of these three objects also have this eleventh property in common. Therefore, probably

• This third object also has this eleventh property in common with the other two.

Of course, in even the best of cases, we have nothing more definite than probability.  Certainty can never be arrived at by using an analogy. Note too, that all the available evidence must be considered if a statement such as that in the third bullet point is to be justified in this way, since there are certain kinds of factors which decrease the probability of the conclusion. Therefore, as with any inductive argument, the requirement to use all available evidence is essential.

According to Lehrer, there are four factors which can affect the probability of any conclusion:

1. The greater the number of objects which have the ten properties in common, the more probable the conclusion becomes.

2. The greater the number of properties which all the objects have in common, the more probable the conclusion becomes.

3. The greater the number of objects that have the ten properties in common but that lack the critical eleventh property, the less probable the conclusion becomes.

4. And most important, the stronger the claim made in the conclusion, relative to the premise, the less probable that conclusion becomes.

Thus Philo, presented with the teleological argument, objected that many complex, machine-like things exist in the universe that have a demonstrably natural cause. The analogy between the universe and machines breaks down because of the third point we just saw above. The philosopher Keith Lehrer, summarizing Philo's argument, wrote:

> We can find intricate order, design, and beauty in a flower, bush, or tree, and all of these are brought about not by an intelligent being but come from a seed in the ground which receives water and sunlight. In none of these four factors— seed, earth, water, sunlight—is there any hint of intelligence. Furthermore, consider a beautiful Persian cat, a peacock, exotic tropic fish, or even a particular human being. The ordering of parts of such organisms, the interrelating functioning of parts, the beauty of many of them are all the causal result of the fertilization of an egg in an act of animal reproduction....What grounds are there for picking one from among four quite different causes of order and design? It is no less reasonable to claim, and therefore no less probable, that the

earth and the other parts of the universe have sprouted from some seed or matured from some egg fertilized eons ago, or some residual part of the instinctive production of some animal long since extinct, than to claim that it is the planned result of some unseen being with great intelligence....because intelligence is only one among many things in this world that produce order and design, there is no reason to think it is any more probable that an intelligent being produced the universe than that one of the other causes of order and design produced the universe.[1]

## Criticism of this "God of the gaps" approach

Neither of these so-called proofs of God's existence as popularized by Aquinas is really proof at all; nor do they convince skeptics. In fact, these "proofs" ultimately fail because, in the final analysis, they are sitting on the demonstrably false assumption of "God of the gaps": explaining the mystery of green goo by invoking God.

Toward the end of the book of Job, God asks Job a series of questions about nature: "do you understand how such and such happens?" Job keeps shaking his head. God's point is not to prove his existence to Job. He is not arguing that "since you don't understand where rain comes from, that means I exist."

Rather, God was responding to Job's doubts about God's *character*: Job could not figure out how to reconcile his suffering with his innocence and was doubting the goodness of God. If Job hadn't done something wrong, then why was he being punished? Was his suffering, in fact, even a consequence of punishment at all? Job's misery, therefore, was leading Job to doubt God was just or

---

[1] Keith Lehrer, *Philosophical Problems and Arguments: An Introduction*, New York: Macmillan Publishing Co., 1974, pp. 374-376

that God even cared. Job *never* wondered if God existed. Job had no doubt about that.

Which itself brings up the interesting point: those who suffer and who believe in God are not commonly the ones who decide that God doesn't exist.  They may get mad at God, but in my experience, many of the most faithful, loving individuals who are most devoted to God turn out to be people who have suffered the most excruciating tragedies.

T.C. Kelly, a man in my church, when asked how he was doing, would respond "I'm too blessed to be stressed" or "I'm blessed all over."  And yet his life had never been an easy one or the sort of existence that many would call happy.  Growing up he had experienced some of the worst horrors of prejudice and hatred, both toward himself and his parents before him. He had suffered the untimely death of his wife after a long illness.  But through it all, he never lost his faith in God.  He devoted himself to helping the hurting, the poor, the down and out, and the otherwise disadvantaged, always convinced of the love of God and his unending goodness and mercy.

It never appeared to bother T.C. that he didn't understand God's plans for him.  He just assumed that God's plans, whatever they might be, were for the best and that God knew what he was doing.

God's response to Job was to show him that there are many things in life that Job couldn't understand, none of which seemed to get in the way of his relationship with God.  How was his inability to explain the current suffering in his life substantively different from his inability to explain how thunder happened?  The question of suffering is simply, according to the argument God makes to Job, no different than *any* questions Job might have regarding the functioning of the universe.  Failure to know the answer to the question of my pain, my tragedy, my anguish does not mean that God doesn't care, or that God is unjust, or even (to ask and answer a question the Bible itself *was not concerned with*) that God does not exist.  All it means is that we have an unanswered question.  One of many, perhaps, and that if we look at the data long enough, we might figure out, just like, over the years, we have figured out how the rain comes, and how thunder happens.

The issue of God's existence throughout the pages of scripture is always simply assumed. No more, no less. Even in those rare passages, such as Psalm 14, where the issue of disbelieving in God is raised, God's existence is not argued.  No proofs for the existence of God are ever offered, nor, in any passage of scripture, is the argument *ever* made that "well, we don't understand this green goo, so it must mean God did it.  Therefore, God really does exist."  The Bible never tries to prove the existence of God.

### Miracles

Miracles are used for the purpose of authenticating the prophetic status of a given individual and to authenticate that the message being given is genuinely of God, rather than simply the imagination of a messenger run amok.  The question of God's existence itself is never at issue.  The issue instead is merely: is this person claiming to be a prophet from God actually one of God's prophets or not?

What about the story of Elijah on Mt. Hermon?  Elijah had a god contest, but the issue again was not, "does God exist?"  Rather, the issue was: *which* god should we worship? *Which* god is able to act? *Which* god matters? *Which* god is most powerful?  *Which* god is worth our allegiance? The issue of whether a deity or deities exist was never at stake.  Everyone already assumed there were gods. Now they had to decide which one was worthy of their attention. The miracle, in its final outcome, merely demonstrated that Yahweh was the better god, a god who actually paid attention to his servant.  This did not stop those who worshipped Baal instead from continuing to worship him; and it did not stop them (as expressed by Jezebel) from attempting to kill Elijah, who worshipped Yahweh instead.  In the Bible, miracles do not seem to be an effective means of convincing unbelievers of much of anything.

What of Jesus and his miracles?  In fact, this failure of miracles to convince the unbelievers is amply illustrated by the reactions to Jesus' miracles by those who failed to follow him or accept him as the long-promised Messiah.  Those who sought to kill Jesus—the religious establishment—were never swayed by his miracles.  They did not seem to doubt that Lazarus had been raised from the dead; they did not seem to question that blind and deaf, ill and demon possessed had been cured by Jesus.  But they still refused to accept Jesus as the Messiah.  It is reminiscent of what Abraham said to the rich man in Hell who requested that Lazarus be sent back to warn his brothers: "If they do not listen to Moses and the prophets, they will not be convinced by a dead man rising to life" (Luke 16:31).  But the question of God's ultimate existence was never at issue.  Doubting God's existence was akin to questioning one's own existence, or the existence of a brother or wife.

The purpose of the prophets, the purpose of those who wrote Scripture, was to interpret the events around them as acts of God.  If no prophet spoke, "thus saith the Lord," no one would be able to tell for sure that the Exodus, or the Babylonian captivity, or any of the other events described in the Bible had anything to do with God.  In fact, even with the prophet to interpret the world for them, people continued to doubt that God had actually acted.

God's existence, in the minds of many, is dependent upon certain proofs or evidences remaining inexplicable by any other means.  They believe that no one must know, *ever*, where the green goo originated.  Only in continued ignorance, if one follows their "logic," can God's existence be considered reasonable and viable. This is the bottom line for the traditional proofs for the existence of God. If we discover some explanation for the goo, God will evaporate. *Explanation* is a ray gun held at the deity's head.

In the exact same way, however, atheism has allowed itself to become just as dependent upon *not understanding.* Only in continuing to believe that there is no adequate explanation for suffering can the atheist's assertion that suffering disproves the existence of God continue to survive. Like the "god of the gaps" so favored by so many believers, the atheist's "ultimate weapon" against God is a fool's weapon, too: a cap gun at best: a "gap means no god" mistake.

So. Many Christians are terrified of explanations. If you can show how the blowing wind moved the water to allow the Israelites to cross the Red Sea as described in Exodus (despite the fact that the author of Exodus says the very thing), many will get mad, suggesting that faith is being undermined, or that you don't believe in God if you accept it. The atheist argues that if an explanation for the beginning of the universe is discovered that shows how perfectly normal physical processes caused the universe to be, then the god predicated upon its eternally remaining a mystery vanishes in a puff. If complexity in biological systems can be explained by purely physical means, then the teleological argument, sometimes called the watchmaker analogy, will also dissolve like Alka-Seltzer in a glass of water.

### Depending on Ignorance

Frankly, to pin one's hopes for the existence of God on what amounts to a bet that we will remain forever ignorant about certain matters, and that we can never, *ever* understand them, strikes me as a bet we are guaranteed to lose, given the historical pattern of the inexplicable becoming explicable. It is, in fact, a serious structural error on the part of Christian theology: we have built our house on a beach below sea level along the Gulf coast of Louisiana and the levees have failed. On top of that, there's a CAT 5 hurricane blowing.

While in an ultimate sense, we believe that God is the final cause, such is not actually a demonstration of God's existence, nor was there *ever* in the biblical picture of things, a felt need for such an argument or demonstration. In the Bible, God's existence was simply assumed.

It is therefore *unnecessary* to try to demonstrate his existence by recourse to some mystery or inexplicable occurrence. Such recourse, ultimately, is bound to be futile, because the universe, being God's to manipulate as easily as we ourselves manipulate it, will always reveal an explanation for whatever happened, happens or will happen, that is in keeping with the laws of physics.

John Derbyshire, of *National Review Magazine*, pointed out in an online posting in December, 2005 that "yes, material causes only are admitted in science, because science is the attempt to find material explanations for observed phenomena. Likewise, only hollow balls 2.5 inches in diameter are allowed in tennis, because tennis is a contest played with 2.5 inch diameter hollow balls. Whether other kinds of balls exist is a matter of opinion among tennis players and fans, I suppose; though if a player were to come on court and attempt to serve a basketball across the net, the rest of us would walk away in disgust."

While the explanation of how rain came was a mystery to the author of the biblical book of Job, it is not a mystery to us. Does our ability to not only explain it, but in some cases to actually make it happen, mean that God has been disproved? Has God further hidden himself in the universe, has he made himself still more inaccessible as we come to gain a better and better understanding of him? Does he shrink as we learn more?  Does he disappear among the baggage?  (1 Samuel 10:20-22)

Or is it rather, perhaps, that the assumption which has moved Christian apologists for these last many centuries, is at its core, flawed and untenable?

There is no need for a ghost in the machine.  Do we look at an engine in our car and ever consider the possibility that there is a small fairy in it who is the real source of its power?  Is there really a demon lurking in our computer that makes the magic happen—or sometimes not?  All joking aside, to postulate such invisible sprites is the babbling nonsense of the insane.  And yet how often do we as Christians do something exactly like this with the universe by our odd arguments?  Does it seem any more sane if we call the ghost in the machine of the universe God rather than an elf?

*It is not that God does not exist.*  What does not need to exist is the assumption that his existence is dependent upon finding something that cannot be explained.  God does not need to be blamed for something in order to exist.  Most Christian apologetics since at least Aquinas has sprung from this same basic mistake: asking questions of the text of scripture that it was not trying to answer.  We have falsely assumed that the existence of the universe in any way makes the existence of God necessary or demonstrable.

### The Unnecessary Deity

God, in the final analysis, even biblically, is "unnecessary" in the sense that a superstitious notion of the functioning of reality is at odds with the biblical picture of reality.  God can always be explained away.

And this is as he wished it, for two reasons.  First, because to assume otherwise lessens him and makes him merely a wonderworker, if God-of-the-gaps theology is right. Secondly, because of the need for freedom.

To find God's hidden cameras watching us would get in the way of what God intends for us to be: free. Just as one is nervous and oppressed when the boss is watching (or a highway patrol car is right behind you on the freeway), or even when dad is watching us play baseball for the first time, so it would be if God were visibly present.

Ask yourself this simple question. Would you rather live in a free country like the United States, or in Nazi Germany being watched by the Gestapo? We believe freedom is a positive good, while totalitarian control is a bad thing. We chafe even when those controlling us are doing it for our benefit, let alone when their motives are questionable. We might all agree that giving money to the Salvation Army Santas at Christmas is a good thing. But do we want to be *forced* to do that good thing? Would it be okay to make us empty our pockets into their buckets whenever we exit a store on threat of incarceration?

Chafing at being told what to do is not a consequence of the Fall; it is not sin, despite some who would like to argue otherwise. It is because God likes freedom and we have that inside us—because freedom is what maximizes, ultimately, God's control. Totalitarianism is what is actively counter to God's will and purpose; not freedom. God gave Adam and Eve a choice (see Genesis 2:15-3:24); God thought it best that they have that choice and that they be free to make the wrong choice. In fact, he thought that their wrong choice and everything that has flowed from that—all of human history—was worth it. He would rather that we be free than that we be good. Freedom was more important than morality, more important than goodness, more important than the life of his Son, more important than preventing all the suffering since that moment. Or else he would never have set up that choice in the first place.

And I think all of this has something to say about the nature of God's sovereignty versus free will. His sovereignty *is* free will. The Soviet experiment with controlled economies failed; and yet a free economy does everything that the Soviets would have wished to see happen in their attempts at control. A paradox, in a way, perhaps (and counter-intuitive), but a failure to reckon with what God himself said about control: Jesus said that the "gentiles" try to lord it over those under them. But among believers, it must not be so: he who would be greatest must be servant of all (Matthew 20:25-28). Submission is mutual, according to Ephesians 5:21. Somehow this all works together. The invisible hand of the free market (to use Adam Smith's phrase), as it were, perhaps serves as one of the best analogies for how God's "sovereignty" actually functions in the universe.

And again, to posit God as a conspiracy or control in the sense that some nut jobs posit conspiracies to explain the workings of the world is probably just as loony as those who believe in the Illuminati.

The argument is made that in order for something as complex as a watch to exist, there must be someone who designed it and built it. On the face of it, that seems a reasonable argument, especially when one remembers that watches indeed have designers and builders.

On the other hand, is a central controller, a firm hand, always necessary in order to get a complex design? Chaos theory points out that randomness, oddly enough, results in very beautiful and elaborate designs or patterns.

One of the best illustrations of how randomness results in order is the modern, free-market economy, which boasts elaborate means of production, distribution and communication systems, all lacking utterly any central control. It is a vey complex design, but without a designer. In fact, those nations who have attempted to centrally control even a portion of their economies have suffered horrid disasters as a result (think of cars such as the Yugo or the East German Trabant, both the product of a socialist, centrally planned system: badly made, unreliable, and hard to get; people in East Germany would wait *years* to get a Trabant).  Countries that have gone full command economy have, without exception, destroyed themselves (Venezuela stands as a recent example.)

But consider this.  In the United States, as an example, if you walk into almost any supermarket, you'll find your favorite candy bar.  You'll discover your favorite flavor of ice cream.  When you visit a car dealer, you have not just one, but hundreds of cars that you can choose from, both new and used, with seemingly infinite varieties of colors and features.  And if, for some odd reason, a given store lacks what you seek, chances are that another store just down the street will have precisely what you're looking for.  In every city in America, you'll be able to find clothing that will fit you, and whose style you'll like.  Worst case scenario: go online and then wait for UPS to deliver it.  Amazon, if no one else, will have it, assuming the thing you want exists at all.

And not only does this system work remarkably well for you personally (so well, in fact, that if you go to McDonalds and order a strawberry shake and they have run out, you're justifiably furious)—it also works for industry as a whole.  Somehow there will be enough nuts and bolts and computer chips in just the right places in all the factories all over the country to manufacture what needs manufacturing.  The infrastructure of the nation is also a marvel of complexity that somehow all works together.  The trucks roll, the trains move, the planes fly, the gasoline and oil, natural gas and electricity, are mostly where and when they need to be.  Your email magically appears in your inbox, no matter where in the world it was sent from.

The question then arises: who designed this complex system?  Who decreed how many boxes of Wheaties would be on your local Walmart's shelves?

The answer, of course, is that there is no single individual in charge of it all.  It grew by itself.  It is an example of how chaos gives rise to order. No one would ever think to argue that all the components of the Wheaties distribution system—from wheat farmers to little cardboard box makers, the printers that printed "Wheaties" and the latest sport hero's picture on the boxes, the manufacturers of printing presses, the orderers of the various colored inks, the makers of those inks, and the people who designed the look of the packaging—had to be in place at once in order for the breakfast of champions to appear on every grocery store shelf.

Aside from Marxists, whose theories are demonstrably unworkable, John Allen Paulos, professor of mathematics at Temple University, points out that all other economists believe that "simple economic exchanges that are beneficial to people become entrenched and then gradually modified as they become part of larger systems of exchange, while those that are not beneficial die out. They accept that Adam Smith's invisible hand brings about the spontaneous order of the modern economy."

And yet, Paulos wonders: why is it then that so many people are reluctant to accept that natural selection and "blind processes" can lead to similar biological order arising spontaneously? Although, he acknowledges that there are significant differences between biological systems and economic systems, he believes we cannot ignore the obvious comparison. Given this reality of economics, Paulos raises a pair of very intriguing questions:

"What would you think of someone who studied economic entities and their interactions in a modern free market economy and insisted that they were, despite a perfectly reasonable and empirically supported account of their development, the consequence of some all-powerful, detail-obsessed economic law-giver? You might deem such a person a conspiracy theorist.

"And what would you think of someone who studied biological processes and organisms and insisted that they were, despite a perfectly reasonable and empirically supported Darwinian account of their development, the consequence of some all-powerful, detail-obsessed biological law-giver?" (ABC News Internet Ventures, 2005)

While this might lead many to decide that there is no God, if we maintain the analogy, or push it just a little, God does not need to vanish in a puff of smoke, with Christians and other monotheists reduced to mad conspiracy theorists on par with those who mutter about chemtrails. But it does, perhaps, have an impact on our understanding of God and his nature, and his relationship with the world.

The key phrase in Paulos's second question is "detail-obsessed" if we take it to mean "micro-managing." Certainly the biblical revelation indicates that God is interested in the details—otherwise why would we want to suggest he pays attention to individual human beings, who are rather minor details in the overall mass of humanity, numbering at present well over seven billion?

One of the puzzles for theologians of a monotheistic bent has been the question of God's sovereignty versus human freedom. From this also comes the question of the issue of human suffering, expressed by the question, "if God is good and all powerful, then why is there sin—why do bad things happen to good people?"

Adam Smith argued for the "invisible hand" of the free market. Of course, this is a metaphor, describing the *outcome* of the free market. What if the very nature of freedom, of the random, is how God is sovereign? What if God gets the Wheaties he wants by setting up, as it were, a free market economy: the world and our subsequent history, as it actually is? In fact, is there any better way for God to get what he wants? Freedom, paradoxically, may maximize God's control. It may indeed be the *means* of his control.

### Conclusion

God exists. That is my assumption. But to point to the unknown and argue, "since I can't explain it, *God* must have done it" is never, in the long run, going to work and really is as silly a statement as pointing to that green goo I began this with and saying, "I don't know where it came from so it must be from God." (and think of how silly you sound if you try to say, "well, although it really came from my sick cat's gut, ultimately God is responsible." Um, sure. I'm feeling more enlightened already.)

God's existence cannot be based on ignorance, any more than his nonexistence may be based on it. The atheist is no more arguing in a reasonable fashion when he points to mystery (such as suffering) and says, "there, you can't answer that, so that means there is no God." To not know is simply to not know. It proves nothing. In fact, to argue that the absence of an answer proves something is to be guilty of the old logical fallacy of *argumentum ad ignorantum*, a favorite of conspiracy theorists and crackpots everywhere.

Do you need to prove that your wife, mother, or father exists? Do you even think about that sort of question? Well, the authors of the Bible never thought about it either when it came to God. The question was never, does God exist, but rather, far more profoundly: who is God—and what does he want of me?

## Chapter Six: The Abundant Life

### We Already Have It

There is no secret to abundant life. We already *have* abundant life (oh *yeah?* Then what about...) The secret, if it is a secret, is that we should believe that God hasn't been lying to us, and that he really, truly *does* know what he is doing, *even* when everything is falling down around our ears.

It was a warm, sunny Friday afternoon in the High Desert of California. The sky was bright and clear, and we were building a new sign for our church. Dandi, one of the women in our church, and I had done most of the work; she had designed the sign and I had cut out all the pieces and she had painted them. Today we were putting the sign in place on its concrete foundation.

At about one o'clock she left with her husband to go to her perfectly normal, ordinary, planned, nothing-special visit with her doctor. She was seven months pregnant. It was supposed to take about an hour and she was hoping to be back before we had finished attaching the sign to the concrete.

About two o'clock, she and her husband returned. I knew right away just from their faces that something was very, very wrong.

The doctor had done an ultrasound and her baby was showing no movement. The amniotic fluid had dropped, and there was no heartbeat. Her baby was dead.

Dandi and her husband went into our pastor's office to give him the news and to talk to him and to pray with him, while my wife and I huddled outside feeling awful.

Something that is obvious, and yet easily forgotten: it is not possible to be fully a part of someone else's grief, no matter how close you might be to them. That night we took them to see a movie and then out to pizza. But of course our minds were not on either the movie or the pizza, and our conversation kept coming back to the fact that Dandi's baby was dead. They would try to induce labor the next week. This had happened on a Friday.

At the end of the evening, they went back to their home to be alone together with their grief, and my wife and I went home to be alone with ours. At church that Sunday, Dandi and her husband were there, and they sang and worshipped and we went out to lunch together.

And the next week was both long and painful.

In the end, Dandi gave birth to a stillborn baby girl, whom she named Marissa Ruth. Ruth is my wife's name. We went with them to the funeral home, helped them make the arrangements, wanting to make certain that in their grief they didn't end up spending more than they needed or wanted. And so on the day of the funeral, we released balloons, and we sang, and we prayed and the baby was buried beneath a tree in the cemetery. Dandi commented that it was like tucking her in for the night.

I wrote a novel a few years ago called *The Wrong Side of Morning*. The title describes the fact that in this day-to-day experience of existence we are living somewhere past midnight, but before the dawn. As Christians we look to a coming city, a coming kingdom, and know on some level that we are pilgrims here, traveling toward the celestial home where we will dwell forever. But we are not there yet.

Our mistake comes in forgetting that this journey we call life is not the destination. And when we make that mistake, as it is oh so easy to make, we grow discouraged and depressed and overwhelmed, because the journey sometimes has potholes, and sometimes we face robbers, and we are wearied by the walk, and the sun is hot, or the wind is cold, or the rain is wet, or the snow gives us frostbite or the mountains seem too steep.

So much of what happens to us seems to make no sense at all, coming upon us without rhyme, reason, or warning.  Someone commented to my wife over lunch at the hospital, while waiting for Dandi to give birth to Marissa, that "you know, good things come to good people, and bad things come to bad people…"  And my wife looked at her lunch companion aghast and asked, "What possible bad thing has Dandi done that it would cost the life of her daughter?"

The disciples of Jesus confronted a blind man one day—a man blind since the day he was born.  They asked a simple question: "Who sinned, this man or his parents?"  And what was Jesus' response?  "Neither."  It was for the glory of God, he told them. (John 9:1-3)

Yet how many still believe what my wife's lunch companion had to say?  This despite the fact that Job's friends had the same opinion, which happened to be the opinion of Satan (a good clue that the friends might be mistaken).  Satan asks the following at the beginning of the book of Job:

"Does Job fear God for nothing?" Satan replied.  "Have you not put a hedge around him and his household and everything he has? You have blessed the work of his hands, so that his flocks and herds are spread throughout the land.  But stretch out your hand and strike everything he has, and he will surely curse you to your face." (Job 1:9-11).

Job's friends ask the same question, with great fear.  If good doesn't come to the good and bad doesn't come to the bad, *then what is the point of being good*?  Job was trying to argue the obvious, yet radical notion that being good or bad doesn't matter.  God treats everyone the same.

Job's friend Eliphaz is horrified and comments: "But you even undermine piety and hinder devotion to God." (Job 15:4)  Why did Eliphaz react that way?  Because from his perspective, the only possible motive for piety was getting a good life. For Eliphaz, God was running a protection racket. "Nice life you have there. Be awful if something bad happened to it." And so Eliphaz dutifully paid.

But if Job was right, then Eliphaz was wasting his money. And worse, there was nothing Eliphaz could do to ensure a life free of pain. He was no longer in control of the outcome of his existence. He had no way of avoiding suffering.

Which is the harsh truth about life that Eliphaz didn't want to face.

Job and God both knew that a blessed life of prosperity is *not* the reason for worshipping God. Satan asks, "Does Job fear God for nothing?" Satan's assumption, the assumption of Job's friends, the assumptions of many Christians and non-Christians alike, *despite* all the evidence in the Bible and in life to the contrary, is that if you do what's right, if you can find the magic spell, if you keep God happy, then you'll be happy and your life will be swell. The fact that life isn't always swell, and many people have the mistaken notion that somehow they are promised swell if they only behave, is part of the reason so many become upset and wonder if God can even exist, since their expectations of what God will do for them are constantly undermined by a harsh reality.

### Perspective

Christians go on believing that the reason they are not happy and "fulfilled" is because there is something wrong with what they are doing. "If only I wasn't screwing up so badly in my life..." If only I could find the right seminar, teacher, preacher, seven-step program, book, video, *then* I would have the answer I'm missing. I just need to know what I'm doing wrong, change it, and start doing it right, and then my life will be wonderful. God is just waiting up there for me to find that secret. Once I do, he'll unleash all the blessings that up till now he's been prevented from sending my way because I'm, well, just too stupid to figure it out.

Of course, this is all nonsense.

Many people have difficulty understanding love and grace. Or just accepting reality.

Stephen Crane, the author of *Red Badge of Courage*, also wrote poetry. In one of his poems, entitled *The Wayfarer*, he speaks of the enormous trouble people have with accepting the truth, however much they may claim they want it:

> The wayfarer,
> Perceiving the pathway to truth,
> Was struck with astonishment.
> It was thickly grown with weeds.
> "Ha," he said,
> "I see that none has passed here
> In a long time."
> Later he saw that each weed
> Was a singular knife.
> "Well," he mumbled at last,
> "Doubtless there are other roads."

Human beings are easily seduced by the wrong roads. There are a lot of them. And most of them are very pretty. The right road is kind of ugly. Instead of truth, people seem mostly to want very tasty lies. The truth tends to taste like castor oil.

Seminars and preaching that are simply a list of things to do, when combined with the promise, either explicit or implicit, that if you just "do these things, you'll be happy and wealthy and your kids will grow up right" turns out to be appealing to the vast majority of people. It is obvious that such legalism tastes great and is less filling to boot. It seems to be what people want and hunger after: it is the meager fantasy that attracts.  Like Jacob, they imagine everything is against them, and so they strive to find things they can *do* that will fix the mess that they see their life as being.  And so teaching about love and grace, by contrast, seems just not practical, just not a solution to what ails them.  Accepting the reality that we are not entirely in control of the outcome of our life scares most of us.  We rebel against the notion that we cannot always prevent bad things from happening to us or our loved ones.  So we embrace legalistic formulas.

Kind of sad, really.  But nothing new.  Paul wrote:

But I am afraid that just as Eve was deceived by the serpent's cunning, your minds may somehow be led astray from your sincere and pure devotion to Christ. For if someone comes to you and preaches a Jesus other than the Jesus we preached, or if you receive a different spirit from the one you received, or a different gospel from the one you accepted, you put up with it easily enough. (2 Corinthians 11:3-4)

And of course the new three- or six- or twelve-part plan to the abundant life doesn't work much longer than the ten week course, or the time it took to read through the books, and yet that rarely cools the desire for the search or that kind of "answer." So, people keep going from this hot thing to the next hot thing, always in search of the list, the word, the promise, the plan that will give them the abundant life.  Few seem ever to consider that perhaps the treadmill that they are on is the actual problem, and that what they really need is simply to get off it altogether.  And what is that treadmill? *The idea that there's something they need to DO.* Or even can do.

The truth is, we already have it—the abundant life— just like Jacob did when he made his complaint.  If we could shift our perspective and stop running about, and lift up our eyes long enough and look at what reality is, from God's perspective, we'd understand that we're just letting people sell our own wallets back to us.  Too easy and too hard, both, despite what Peter writes:

> His divine power has given us everything we need for life and godliness through our knowledge of him who called us by his own glory and goodness.  Through these he has given us his very great and precious promises, so that through them you may participate in the divine nature and escape the corruption in the world caused by evil desires. (2 Peter 1:3-4)

People are always pleased to find something which tells them that they can have a better life if only they do three simple things, or even three hard things. Unfortunately, reality is something else altogether, even in the land of ministry and serving God.  I read so many books where authors give examples of people having "successful" ministries as a consequence of saying a special prayer, or learning a certain lesson, or following some program. And what is a successful ministry?  One where a lot of people get involved, one where there are lots of converts.  And certainly, lots of people getting saved, lots of people getting involved, lots of money being raised are good things.  But success is not necessarily a matter of numbers.  There's nothing wrong with numbers, but it doesn't always work that way.  And not having the numbers doesn't mean that you've done something wrong.

There needs to be an understanding that simply doing God's will is a success in and of itself; that having a relationship with God, that loving him and loving people is all that is asked and that there are no guarantees that you will see anyone saved, any ministries grow, any increase in growth either spiritually, in numbers, or in money.  It could all go south on you.  After all, look at the prophet Jeremiah as an obvious example: in his lifetime, no one paid attention to him and he kept getting thrown in prison. Or how about Isaiah?  According to tradition, Manasseh stuffed him in a log and sawed him in two lengthwise.

We need to take seriously what the author of Ecclesiastes wrote:

> I have seen something else under the sun:
> The race is not to the swift
> or the battle to the strong,
> nor does food come to the wise
> or wealth to the brilliant
> or favor to the learned;
> but time and chance happen to them all.
> Moreover, no man knows when his hour will come:
> As fish are caught in a cruel net,
> or birds are taken in a snare,
> so men are trapped by evil times that fall unexpectedly upon them. (Ecclesiastes 9:11-12)

In the early church, all the leaders but John were killed for their faith.  When John wrote the book of Revelation, as near as he could see, everything he'd spent his life on, everything that mattered to him, was wrecked.  Everyone he loved and cared about was either dead or gone: his family was wiped out, Jerusalem was a smoldering ruin, the temple of God was destroyed.  A very odd way, it seemed to him, for God to be treating his servants.

Hebrews 11 ends by pointing out that many of the great people of faith never received the promise; from their perspective, everything did not work out:

Others were tortured and refused to be released, so that they might gain a better resurrection. Some faced jeers and flogging, while still others were chained and put in prison. They were stoned; they were sawed in two; they were put to death by the sword. They went about in sheepskins and goatskins, destitute, persecuted and mistreated—the world was not worthy of them. They wandered in deserts and mountains, and in caves and holes in the ground. These were all commended for their faith, yet none of them received what had been promised. (Hebrews 11:35b-39)

Does that mean that God doesn't want us to be happy? Does that mean he wants to see us fail and fail and fail and to be forever miserable?

Of course not. Paul writes, "I have learned to be content whatever the circumstances." (Philippians 4:11)

What it means is that we need to reevaluate what it is that we value.

A teacher approached Jesus once and asked him, "what is the greatest commandment?" Jesus' response is profound. He told the teacher that the greatest commandment was to love God. Then Jesus said there is a second commandment that is equal to it and complements it: "love your neighbor as yourself." Jesus explained that those two commandments contain everything that the Bible is all about. It is the Bible's theme. Later, Paul makes the same point in Romans 13: "The commandments, 'Do not commit adultery,' 'Do not murder,' 'Do not steal,' 'Do not covet,' and whatever other commandment there may be, are summed up in this one rule: 'Love your neighbor as yourself.' Love does no harm to its neighbor. Therefore, love is the fulfillment of the law." In fact, Jesus tells a parable that explains that loving people in fact is how we show our love to God (Matthew 25:31-46); the apostle John will reiterate this point as well (1 John 4:7-21).

So, what does this mean for us? We need to think again of what loving God and loving people means in the context of our lives. We need to remind ourselves to think of the nature of faith and freedom, of grace and peace. And most of all, we need to catch our breath, open our eyes, and really take a look at reality afresh. We need a new *perspective*. We need to realize that what God asks us to see is the world through *his* eyes, to see our lives through *his* eyes, to realize that because we love him and he loves us, and through us, we love others, that we have joy and satisfaction and success, even in the midst of the gloom and apparent failure that surrounds us.  There is no secret to abundant life; we *have* abundant life.  The secret, if it is a secret, is just that we have to believe that God hasn't been lying to us, and that he really and truly does know what he is doing, even when everything is crashing down around our ears. Like Jacob, we need to find out what our situation really is, not just what a limited point of view tries to make us think it is.

I keep thinking about why so often we are told to "encourage one another" in the Bible.  If life was really guided by our fidelity to a seven-part program that promises abundant peaceful living, I don't think we'd need that constant reminder to encourage.

Instead of an easy plan, a simple set of principles, life is hard and what we see around us can confuse us and throw us off balance.  I need constant reminding that the world is not really spinning around me out of control.  My dizziness is temporary and subjective, after all.  And so I make a conscious choice to be reminded of that bit of non-dizzy reality.

## Chapter Seven: The Real Question

*What is the real question?*  The traditional question regarding suffering, the question of the modern world is, "if God is good, loving and all powerful, then why is there sin and suffering?"

This is essentially the opposite question to the one we should be asking.  If humanity is in a fallen state, having made a poor choice, and if God has granted us freedom and hides himself so that he may always be explained away, why is there anything good in the world?

When something goes right for us, we never ask "why me?" *We only ask it if something bad happens.*

That may be natural for us in our current condition, but it is the opposite of what we should be asking.  Because we believed God was holding out on us—Eve was convinced that God, in forbidding the one tree, was withholding something beneficial—in our hearts we really don't believe God is good or loving. We do not trust him.  We do not believe he wants what is best for us.  We believe that God wants us to do the last thing we'd ever want to do and to somehow be grateful for it.  We expect to suffer because "it's good for us" like getting a shot or swallowing cod liver oil. "We had dirt to eat and we were thankful," is the attitude we imagine for the life we believe God intends for us.

We expect things to go wrong because we believe that God wants to teach us a lesson and that what he thinks is best for us is in fact something that will make us miserable.

We believe that if we ask for bread, God will give us a scorpion (Luke 11:9-13). We don't trust him.  So, the other part of the *real* question is also, *why don't we trust God?*

Children tend to think this way regarding their parents. They are quick to assume malevolence on our part: that we deny giving them what they ask for simply because we're mean or don't want them to have fun, or simply don't want to be bothered.

Given our cynicism with the people in our lives, even our loved ones, is it any surprise what our attitude is with God? My wife or daughter says to me "I love you" and I immediately become suspicious, especially if they add "do you love me?"  Then I know for sure they just want something: usually money.

And so we tend to imagine God's attitude toward us may be the same attitude we have regarding our own children.  We pray, God looks at the caller ID, and just rolls his eyes.

Except.

Look at Matthew 7:7-12 (and its parallel in Luke):

> "Ask and it will be given to you; seek and you will find; knock and the door will be opened to you. For everyone who asks receives; the one who seeks finds; and to the one who knocks, the door will be opened.
>
> "Which of you, if your son asks for bread, will give him a stone? Or if he asks for a fish, will give him a snake? If you, then, though you are evil, know how to give good gifts to your children, how much more will your Father in heaven give good gifts to those who ask him! So in everything, do to others what you would have them do to you, for this sums up the Law and the Prophets."

"Even though you are evil…" we give our children the money they ask for if we have it or can somehow manage to scrounge it up.  And we answer our phones even though we recognize the incoming number.  God is not like us.  He is better than us.  He always has our best interests in mind.  He never rolls his eyes.  He's never just "worn out" or "too tired" or "too broke."

People tend to assume malevolence on God's part: he's mad at me, he wants me to learn a hard lesson, suffering builds character, he just doesn't like me, his plans are different than mine and I just need to suck it up and be thankful for dirt, even though I wanted ice cream.

The skeptic, on the other hand, looks at this and sees madness: we're playing mind games and refusing to face reality—and thus concludes that suffering, being a bad thing, proves either that God is sadistic—and hence all the angry atheists—or, that obviously there is no God at all, we're playing make believe—and thus relieving us of having to suffer the delusion of an angry, sadistic, or uncaring deity and so freeing us to live without fear that we are about to be walloped by God's hickory stick.

Of course, it also frees us to be orphans.

If the Kingdom of Heaven is better than this world, then how can this be the best of all possible worlds?  But, as I asked before, what if the Kingdom of Heaven can come about only because of this world: that is, the Kingdom of Heaven requires this world and this world creates the Kingdom of Heaven: the Kingdom of Heaven is a *consequence* of this world. It grows from this world: in fact, it is not entirely—or even at all—separate from this world.

Some may object to this for various reasons, but consider: without the inhabitants of this world, there can be no next world, no kingdom of heaven.  We—the church, the people of this world are what make up the Kingdom! So yes, this world creates the next world in that it creates the people who make it up: after all, the bride of Christ, the celestial city of Jerusalem coming to Earth from heaven is what? The people of God (see Rev. 21:9 where the author explicitly identifies the celestial city of Jerusalem as "the bride, the wife of the Lamb"; see also Rev. 21:2). The question here is: *what is the kingdom of Heaven?*

The short answer: it is God's people.  Therefore, this world is necessary for the kingdom of Heaven to exist—and so this then *is* the best of all possible worlds—it is the only way the better world of the kingdom comes about—which is paradoxical unless you realize that the kingdom is co-existent with this world.

And, in fact, this is explicit: the kingdom in a very real sense is now.

It is precisely what Jesus said:

> Once, having been asked by the Pharisees when the kingdom of God would come, Jesus replied, "The kingdom of God does not come with your careful observation, nor will people say, 'Here it is,' or 'There it is,' because the kingdom of God is within you." (Luke 17:20-21)

When we ask, "is this the best of all possible worlds?" we must recognize that this world *includes* the Kingdom.

Ask yourself this when you peer at Jesus sleeping in the manger, "is this baby the best of all possible human beings?"  The baby is no less Jesus than the resurrected Lord.  This world is the baby to the adult that is the Kingdom of God.

Consider, too, that even the death of the righteous—what most would consider an example of the core problem in the issue of suffering being unjust and an affront to the existence of God—is, counterintuitively, considered to be a positive good, a blessing even, based on a few biblical passages:

> The righteous perish,
> and no one takes it to heart;
> the devout are taken away,
> and no one understands
> that the righteous are taken away

to be spared from evil.
Those who walk uprightly
enter into peace;
they find rest as they lie in death. (Isaiah 57:1-2)

Precious in the sight of the LORD
is the death of his faithful servants. (Psalm
116:15)

"As for you, go back home. When you set foot in
your city, the boy will die. All Israel will mourn
for him and bury him. He is the only one
belonging to Jeroboam who will be buried,
because he is the only one in the house of
Jeroboam in whom the LORD, the God of Israel,
has found anything good. (1 Kings 14:12-13)

Love is the core of the Bible. Jesus pointed out that it
was on the twin commandments, to love God and to love
people, that the whole Bible hung (Matthew 22:34-40).
Paul emphasizes it in his writing, too. He explained that all
the commandments in the Bible could be summarized with
a single commandment: "love your neighbor as yourself"
(Romans 13:9 and Galatians 5:14). This concept is also a
core concept in Judaism. The story is told of a Rabbi who
was forced, on pain of death, to recite the entire Torah
while standing on one foot. His response was to say "Love
the Lord your God with all your heart, mind and soul and
love your neighbor as yourself. All the rest is
commentary."

Because of love, Christians should be the most
optimistic of people. The way of the world is to be
gloomy, to always expect the worst, to believe that
ultimately there is no hope. The *world* embraces
pessimism.

The reason we keep going in the face of problems, in the face of setbacks, in the face of discouragement and nothing going right is precisely because of this thing called love. We keep our zeal, our spiritual fervor, we keep on serving the Lord because we know God loves us. And his love inspires us to love the people around us, and to press on.

Think about how a young man or woman feel in the first throws of love. Nothing else matters. The world is beautiful and all is right with the world. Nothing else matters as long as he or she is loved and loves in return.

That's what our relationship with God can do for us. That's the power of true love.

What did Paul write about grief, about how we react when someone dies? Not that we aren't sad, but that we "do not grieve like the rest of mankind, who have no hope" (1 Thessalonians 4:13). Because we know God loves us, we can face the worst without despair.

We understand that things will work out for our good. As Paul wrote, "I am convinced that neither death nor life, neither angels nor demons, neither the present nor the future, nor any powers, neither height nor depth, nor anything else in all creation, will be able to separate us from the love of God that is in Christ Jesus our Lord." (Romans 8:38-39)

## Why Should I Even Bother Getting Up in the Morning?

I don't know about you, but sometimes I get really discouraged and down.

Life has a lot of problems. After the lawsuit against us was gone, after we adopted our children, did life suddenly become a bed of roses?

Well, sometimes things are good, and sometimes not. For instance, our youngest daughter was exposed to many illicit drugs before she was born. She was diagnosed with ADHD by the time she was three; she required physical and developmental therapy.  She had multiple counselors.  She went to special preschools and kindergarten.

And then, when she was fourteen, she became increasingly psychotic.  She turned violent, regularly breaking things in our house, punching and kicking holes in our walls, breaking windows, and eventually repeatedly hitting me, giving me black eyes, and even drawing blood.

Eventually she was diagnosed with severe bipolar disorder.  After being briefly arrested, going homeless for a few days, she was finally hospitalized twice. Thanks to those hospitalizations and the work of her psychologist and psychiatrist, she finally stabilized about the age of nineteen when she got the right cocktail of medications.

The violence has ended. But she remains very immature and incapable of living on her own; she still tends to make poor choices and has difficulty maintaining relationships—and most of her relationships—though they are short—are with people that only take advantage of her. She remains difficult and a source of stress and anxiety. But slowly she is maturing, growing, improving.

People tell me that I should read the Bible when I get down; that it can help me feel better.  So, let's pretend that when I woke up this morning, I wondered what the point was to my life, and questioned why should I even get out of bed this morning?

So I open my Bible and turn to Ecclesiastes chapter one:

> The words of the Teacher, son of David, king in
> Jerusalem:
> "Meaningless! Meaningless!"
> says the Teacher.
> "Utterly meaningless!
> Everything is meaningless."

Okay, let's go on through the rest of the first chapter:

What does man gain from all his labor
at which he toils under the sun?
Generations come and generations go,
but the earth remains forever.
The sun rises and the sun sets,
and hurries back to where it rises.
The wind blows to the south
and turns to the north;
round and round it goes,
ever returning on its course.
All streams flow into the sea,
yet the sea is never full.
To the place the streams come from,
there they return again.
All things are wearisome,
more than one can say.
The eye never has enough of seeing,
nor the ear its fill of hearing.
What has been will be again,
what has been done will be done again;
there is nothing new under the sun.
Is there anything of which one can say,
"Look! This is something new"?
It was here already, long ago;
it was here before our time.
There is no remembrance of men of old,
and even those who are yet to come
will not be remembered
by those who follow.

I, the Teacher, was king over Israel in Jerusalem. I
devoted myself to study and to explore by wisdom
all that is done under heaven. What a heavy
burden God has laid on men! I have seen all the

things that are done under the sun; all of them are meaningless, a chasing after the wind.

What is twisted cannot be straightened;
what is lacking cannot be counted.

I thought to myself, "Look, I have grown and increased in wisdom more than anyone who has ruled over Jerusalem before me; I have experienced much of wisdom and knowledge." Then I applied myself to the understanding of wisdom, and also of madness and folly, but I learned that this, too, is a chasing after the wind.
For with much wisdom comes much sorrow;
the more knowledge, the more grief.

Um.  Okay. So maybe not so encouraging?  Maybe disturbing, or even confusing?

If you have a broken leg, it is improbable that someone will tell you to "read the Bible" or "pray" in order to fix it. Instead, they will urge you to visit a doctor.  Same thing if you are paralyzed and confined to a wheelchair.  No one will suggest you get your lazy ass out of the chair.  They probably won't try to make you feel guilty for sitting down all the time.  It is improbable that they would suggest "why don't you just snap out of it?"

No one tells a diabetic, "You're weak because you are dependent upon insulin."  No one is likely to condemn you for taking high blood pressure medication or argue that if you "got the sin out of your life" you could forgo your dependency on pharmaceuticals.

If you suffer depression you cannot just snap out of it any more than you can just snap out of a stroke.  Your brain is broken (like any other organ in your body, your brain can stop functioning properly).  There are a wide range of illnesses that can affect how you think, how you perceive the world. Get medical help for it!  All the self-help books, all the words of encouragement, all the praying, will never solve the problem for you.  You need a doctor just as badly as if you had cancer.  And, like cancer, depression is potentially a fatal illness.  It certainly is debilitating.

What about those words in Ecclesiastes?  Ecclesiastes is not a cheerful book.

But. Ecclesiastes really does have a positive message for us. It's just easy to miss, obviously.

Ecclesiastes is a weird book of the Bible that we don't usually think of reading to make us feel better about ourselves or anything else—so how does it work?  What's Ecclesiastes for?  Why is it in the Bible?  What was God thinking?

Consider an analogy.  A hammer is not particularly useful for sawing lumber.  Screwdrivers make rather poor paperclips.  There are a variety of tools for a variety of needs.  Likewise, not every passage of the Bible is designed to solve the same needs.  1 Chronicles chapters 1-9 are not likely to be useful in evangelism.  Genesis 1 has nothing to say about how to perform a sacrifice in the temple in Jerusalem during the time of Solomon.

Although Ecclesiastes is rarely preached or taught from, it probably matches the overall culture of the modern western world, and speaks to its issues better than just about any other section of the Bible.  It matches the twenty-first century outlook on life which affirms YOLO—"you only live once" and "just do it."  Ecclesiastes is for those who are grabbing all that life has to offer, who are mass consumers. It speaks at the niggling voice that murmurs in our ears at 1:00 in the morning when we are having trouble sleeping.

It is also a book that one must be careful with.  Missing the context of a biblical passage is always a problem, as it is with any bit of writing or literature; certainly politics makes a sport from the out of context sound bite.

Ecclesiastes lends itself to this sort of abuse/disuse more that most parts of the Bible. I've had fun with this sort of thing—as I think most Christians have with various bits of the Bible as asking such questions as, what sort of car did Jesus drive? "They were all in one Accord" as the joke goes.

Or who is the shortest man in the Bible?

Is it Knee-high-miah? (Nehemiah 1:1)

Bildad the shuhite? (Job 2:11)

Or Peter, since he slept on his watch? (Matthew 26:40)

My roommate in college was particularly enamored of Psalm 37:37 in the KJV translation: "Mark the perfect man." Since his name is Mark.

Then there's my life verse, Ecclesiastes 10:19:

A feast is made for laughter,
and wine makes life merry,
but money is the answer for everything.

What is disturbing, besides the nihilism, is that even if you read the verses around it, it is hard to fit what it's saying into conformity with the rest of the Bible or standard Christian thinking about the meaning and purpose of life. After all, if money is the answer for everything, then how can loving it be the root of all evil?

And so as we face the Book of Ecclesiastes as a whole, there are some things to keep in mind, to understand about it, so that you'll "get" what's going on, so that even my "life verse" will make sense in the broader context of scripture.

First, it is an extended argument—that is, the author has a point he's trying to make and if you don't pay close attention to the whole thing—well, it would be like trying to make sense of the movie Memento if you only pulled a scene or two out of it. Or like trying to make sense of the story line in Lost without seeing all of it—or, you know, take your pick of any rather convoluted series on TV today or in recent history.

Second, the point the author is trying to make at first will seem awful and anti-Christian.  That is, the author is arguing that life has no meaning: it is ultimately absurd and pointless and any meaning it has comes from what you decide to make of it.

For those with a more philosophic bent, you might recognize that this is very similar to existentialism, a philosophical system that argues that life has no intrinsic meaning.  It has meaning only as we decide to give it meaning.  Life's meaning or purpose is individual, belonging only to you.  Life in existential thought is absurd.  Thus, because life has zero real meaning or purpose, it is absurd to imagine that it is unfair.  Why do bad things happen to good people?  For the existentialist, the very concept of "goodness" or "badness" are absurd and meaningless.  Whatever happens just happens and is just as meaningless as everything else.  Shit happens, as the bumper sticker announces.  It might as well happen to a good person as a bad one.  No "one" cares.  It is all part of the absurdity, meaninglessness, and emptiness of it all.

So now you might be wondering at this point, why would God put something like existentialist philosophy in the Bible?  Doesn't it run counter to everything the Bible is about, everything he wants us to know?  Doesn't God believe life has meaning apart from whatever subjectively might matter to us?

Certainly, though perhaps one could move the existentialist point of view back a stage, to God, and argue that to God, existence is meaningful only because he has chosen to make it so.

And I have only given you *part* of the point the author of Ecclesiastes is trying to make.

The author of Ecclesiastes is indeed arguing that life has no meaning; he affirms it is ultimately absurd, and pointless, and he believes that any meaning comes from an individual's own decision—*assuming* that God doesn't care to interact with his creatures and has not bothered to reveal himself to us.

See, the ultimate point—the non-absurdity—of the book of Ecclesiastes is that it demonstrates the need for something like the Bible in the first place. The author is going to explain that if all we had to go on was what we can figure out from life the universe and everything, then God is unknowable, the meaning to life is unknowable, and life is thus obviously absurd and pointless. *"Meaningless"* Ecclesiastes' author would—and does—argue. And he sets it all up for us in the very beginning of his philosophic treatise, his essay on life as something absurd.

So, some additional preliminaries now to help us find our way through this dark forest, this gloomy jungle of an essay, this valley of the shadow of death.

How do we learn about God? That is, what is the source for information about him? If God exists, then he should, in some way, be accessible. We should be able to find out things about him. But how? One way is called "general revelation."

General revelation refers to that information that comes from the universe around us and from history (see Psalm 19:1-6, Romans 1:19-20, Psalm 8:13, Isaiah 40:12-14, 26, Acts 14:15-17, 17:24- 28)  It reveals, or informs us on such matters as the wisdom, power, and glory of God (Romans 1:20).  How so?

One thing that should be pointed out before we go much further. Religion in general, and Christianity in particular, are criticized in what amounts to a strawman argument sort of way by claiming that religion, or Christianity, are built upon "revelation" which is not evidence based unlike say science. This is derived from a misunderstanding of what the term "revelation" means in a theological setting. The term is used very technically to describe the source of information—whatever information we may have—whether it comes from everything around us, as in the case of general revelation, or whether it comes from God more directly, which is then described with the technical term "special revelation." An analogy might help clarify the concept.  One can gain information about an author by reading her works, talking to or corresponding with people who knew the author, visiting the author's birthplace, schools, workplaces and home and rifling through her things and examining her receipts and the books on her shelves, the magazines and newspapers she subscribed to and the like.  This could be likened to what is meant by "general revelation" in the sorts of information gathering that can be done to learn about God.  Or, one can learn about an author by corresponding with her, or by interviewing her, or by becoming her friend or lover.  This would be akin to what theologians mean when they talk about "special revelation."

Another analogy would be to think about how archeology works.  We have an idea about the civilization and lives of pre-literate peoples based on what they've left behind of their lives: the trash (fish bones, scraps of food and wood, shells and the like), firepits, ashes, entombed or buried bodies, jewelry, clay pots, artworks, and the like.

In much the same way, if we have posited a creator for the universe, then the universe itself should tell us something about its creator.  Such information, like the information from scattered leavings of ancient pre-literate peoples, is going to be limited.  Better, and far happier for archeologists is when they discover texts—when the civilization is literate and examples of their literacy have survived.  These ancient texts are far more informative and give us far greater detail than can be gleaned from piles of trash and pottery.  Our understanding of civilizations that have left written records are far greater than for those which have not.  Even better would be to interview such ancient people, to visit them in their time (as would occur if we had access to time machines.)

In learning about God, this equivalent of texts and interview is given the technical designation "special revelation."

In the sense of how Christianity understands it and uses it, the term "special revelation" refers to information about God that comes by means of miracles, direct communication, the incarnation (Jesus—that is God—when he came as a human being to the planet), and finally, through scripture.  Scripture is the principle way by which God currently reveals (or discloses) himself to human beings, and for Christian theologians becomes the final judge and arbiter, the final authority of all such communication, general or special.

So what are the weaknesses or limitations on our sources of information about God?  Both have lacunae with regard to the data that can be gained from them. With regard to general revelation, the author of Ecclesiastes attempts to arrive at an understanding of God and at an understanding of the purpose of human existence, apart from God's self-disclosure in the Bible and apart from any attempt to talk to or converse with the Creator.  The author of Ecclesiastes fails to come to a clear understanding of what God expects, leading him to futility and despair: he concludes, based on the evidence he could find from life, the universe, and everything, that bad things happen to good people, good things happen to bad people.  There is nothing for human beings but to be terrified at a capricious God and universe.

His conclusions in many ways are little different from that of modern existentialism, except for existentialism's atheism.

That said, the theism of Ecclesiastes does not really differ so much, practically speaking, from the atheism inherent in existentialism, since the God of Ecclesiastes has no real impact on the life of the book's author.  The God of Ecclesiastes is at best transcendent and unconcerned with the lives of his creatures, and at worst, malevolently inclined.  General revelation is unlikely to reveal much in the way of the attitudes and feelings of God, or of his expectations, if any, for his creatures, or whether he is concerned about them.  Just as an archeologist would have no strong evidence of what an ancient, pre-literate society's language, religious beliefs, stories or culture might actually be.  And when it comes to authors and understanding them from what they have written, Larry Niven's comment to someone who criticized him based on the attitudes and beliefs of a character in one of his novels: "We authors have a technical term for readers who confuse the beliefs of a character with that of its author: 'idiot.'"

If general revelation has limitations or weaknesses, what about special revelation?  Is it also limited?  Does it also suffer from weaknesses?

But of course!

Keeping with the archeology analogy. K.A. Kitchen (Egyptologist from University of Liverpool, England) wrote in *The Bible in Its World*, that when it come to our knowledge of ancient times, it works like this: about ten percent of the ancient world survives buried around us to the present time.  Of that, about ten percent has been surveyed—that is, we know where some stuff is buried.  Of that, about ten percent has actually been excavated to some extent or other.  And of that, about ten percent has been published.  We know the ancient world as well as we could learn about our surroundings if limited to staring at it through a soda straw.

Special revelation is sufficient, not complete or exhaustive.  It does not tell us everything there is to know about God or the universe.  Christian theologians will be quick to point out that the Bible, an example of special revelation, has serious limitations.  It does not even attempt to answer all the questions we might have about God.  As interested as we are in how old the universe is and exactly how it came to be, those were not questions that the biblical writers tried to answer.  We are very curious about the devil, what motivates him, where he came from.  The biblical authors never attempted to answer either of those modern questions, either.  The Bible does not provide medical or scientific information; it does not offer a cure for cancer or bipolar disorder; it does not discuss how one might prevent or cure infections.  There is nothing within its pages about dark matter, dark energy, or whether string theory is ever going to be testable.  It offers no theories regarding quantum gravity.  Neither will a reader find solutions for poverty or any discussions regarding what so focuses our attentions regarding the latest issues in politics or who to vote for or against.  There is not a bit of information in the Bible about how to repair a carburetor or how to get the sound to work on one's cellphone.  The Bible does not offer an answer to how best to govern a nation or what sort of economic policies are preferable.  It gives us no solutions for poverty or homelessness, or how to stop oppression, aggression, or war. There are no hidden cures for cancer or mental illness in the pages of the Bible.

Thus, general revelation has its role to play, just as special revelation does.  But both are only limited vessels of information, neither able to offer complete guidance or answers to every possible conundrum.  Those who tell you that they know the answers for every problem, especially the ones that so vex and concern you, are just trying to sell you something or get control over you.

## Chapter Eight: Toward an Answer

Fyodor Dostoevsky, the Russian novelist, is well known for a certain line of questioning that occurs in his novel, the *Brothers Karamazov* (published 1879), that sets up the modern question of suffering and whether the existence of God is compatible with such a world in a very clear and memorable fashion with a dialog between two of the brothers:

> "Listen! I took the case of children only to make my case clearer. Of the other tears of humanity with which the earth is soaked from its crust to its center, I will say nothing. I have narrowed my subject on purpose. I am a bug, and I recognize in all humility that I cannot understand why the world is arranged as it is. Men are themselves to blame, I suppose; they were given paradise, they wanted freedom, and stole fire from heaven, though they knew they would become unhappy, so there is no need to pity them. With my pitiful, earthly, Euclidian understanding, all I know is that there is suffering and that there are none guilty; that cause follows effect, simply and directly; that everything flows and finds its level—but that's only Euclidian nonsense, I know that, and I can't consent to live by it! What comfort is it to me that there are none guilty and that cause follows effect simply and directly, and that I know it? I must have justice, or I will destroy myself. And not justice in some remote infinite time and space, but here on earth, and that I could see myself. I have believed in it. I want to see it, and if I am dead by then, let me rise again, for if it all happens without me, it will be too

unfair. Surely I haven't suffered simply that I, my crimes and my sufferings, may manure the soil of the future harmony for somebody else. I want to see with my own eyes the hind lie down with the lion and the victim rise up and embrace his murderer. I want to be there when everyone suddenly understands what it has all been for. All the religions of the world are built on this longing, and I am a believer. But then there are the children, and what am I to do about them? That's a question I can't answer. For the hundredth time I repeat, there are numbers of questions, but I've only taken the children, because in their case what I mean is so unanswerably clear. Listen! If all must suffer to pay for the eternal harmony, what have children to do with it, tell me, please? It's beyond all comprehension why they should suffer, and why they should pay for the harmony. Why should they, too, furnish material to enrich the soil for the harmony of the future? I understand solidarity in sin among men. I understand solidarity in retribution, too; but there can be no such solidarity with children. And if it is really true that they must share responsibility for all their fathers' crimes, such a truth is not of this world and is beyond my comprehension. Some jester will say, perhaps, that the child would have grown up and have sinned, but you see he didn't grow up, he was torn to pieces by the dogs, at eight years old. Oh, Alyosha, I am not blaspheming! I understand, of course, what an upheaval of the universe it will be when everything in heaven and earth blends in one hymn of praise and everything that lives and has lived cries aloud: 'Thou art just, O Lord, for Thy ways are revealed.' When the mother embraces the fiend who threw her child to the dogs, and all three cry aloud with tears, 'Thou art just, O Lord!' then, of course, the crown of knowledge will be reached and all will be made clear. But what pulls me up here is that I can't accept that harmony. And while I am on earth, I make haste to take my own measures. You see, Alyosha, perhaps it really may happen that if I live to that moment, or rise again to see it, I, too, perhaps, may cry aloud with the rest, looking at the mother embracing the child's torturer, 'Thou art just, O Lord!' but I don't want to cry aloud then. While there is still time, I hasten to protect myself, and so I renounce the higher harmony altogether. It's not worth the tears of that one tortured child who beat itself on the breast with its little fist and prayed in its stinking outhouse, with its unexpiated tears to 'dear, kind God!' It's not worth it, because those tears are unatoned for. They must be atoned for, or there can be no harmony. But how? How are you going to atone for them? Is it possible? By their being avenged? But what do I care for avenging them? What do I care for a hell for oppressors? What good can hell do, since those children have already been tortured? And what becomes of harmony, if there is hell? I want to forgive. I want to embrace. I don't want more suffering. And if the sufferings of children go to swell the sum of sufferings which was necessary to pay for truth, then I protest that the truth is not worth such a price. I don't want the mother to embrace the oppressor who threw her son to the dogs! She dare not forgive him! Let her forgive him for herself, if she will, let her forgive the torturer for the immeasurable suffering of her mother's heart. But the sufferings of her tortured child she has no right to forgive; she dare not forgive the torturer, even if the child were to forgive him! And if that is so, if they dare not forgive, what becomes of harmony? Is there in the whole world a being who would have the right to forgive and could forgive? I don't want harmony. From love for humanity I don't want it. I would rather be left with the unavenged suffering. I would rather remain with my unavenged suffering and unsatisfied indignation, even if I were wrong. Besides, too high a price is asked for harmony; it's beyond our means to pay so much to enter on it."

And the famous bit:

"Tell me yourself, I challenge your answer. Imagine that you are creating a fabric of human destiny with the object of making men happy in the end, giving them peace and rest at last, but that it was essential and inevitable to torture to death only one tiny creature—that baby beating its breast with its fist, for instance—and to found that edifice on its unavenged tears, would you consent to be the architect on those conditions? Tell me, and tell the truth."

"No, I wouldn't consent," said Alyosha softly.

"And can you admit the idea that men for whom you are building it would agree to accept their happiness on the foundation of the unexpiated blood of a little victim? And accepting it would remain happy for ever?"

"No, I can't admit it."

And so the problem could not be much more clearly presented. If God is good, if God is loving, and if God is powerful, then why does such suffering exist? Why do such horrors go on and on? Why is there no immediate accounting, no intervention to stop or prevent these awful things from happening?

The answer thus far boils down to the simple statement that the question, though begging of an answer, does not demonstrate atheism is the only possible answer, nor does it demonstrate that Christians are stupid. It is only an unanswered question. One cannot legitimately assert that a failure to answer the question means "ah ha, there is no God" anymore than a failure of an atheist to explain where the Big Bang came from means that "there is a God." *Argumentum ad ignorantum* never works out well. Not being able to answer a question does not mean there isn't an answer. The failure of one's opponent being able to answer the question does not mean that one's preferred answer must be right, and his ignorance is not evidence in support of your rightness. If he doesn't know the answer to 2 and 2 is what, that does not make you right when you say, "ah ha, the answer therefore has to be 42." Nor does your answer of "42" become correct just because you are correct that your opponent's answer "7" is incorrect.

So we have discussed whether or not the question at hand is even a legitimate question, or if it suffers from the problem of the question in Douglas Adams' *Hitchhiker's Guide to the Galaxy* which offered that the answer actually is "42" but there's a problem with the question in that the *question* is not quite the right one.

The question behind the question as formulated—why do bad things happen to good people, if God is good and powerful—is simply the thought that we do not deserve to suffer; we have not done anything bad enough to justify the horror that has befallen us. The suffering of our lives, our ultimate death, is not proportional punishment to what we have done. On top of that is another question: why can I do nothing to alter what happens to me? Why am I not in control of my life? I should be able to control what happens to me.

We suffer from superstitious thinking; we suffer from what afflicted Job's friends.  We think that whatever happens to us should be what I made happen to us.  If I'm good, then good things should happen.  If I'm bad, then bad things should happen.  There should be a clear-cut cause and effect relationship.  Sort of like imagining that a heart shaped leaf on a plant should mean that the plant will be beneficial to my heart.

What is upsetting to us is that we do not have a way of controlling the outcome of our lives.  We simply are not really in control at all and that is utterly terrifying.

In the final season of The Big bang theory, Sheldon Cooper's and Amy Farrah Fowler's wedding was delayed—that is, they got to it late—as they worked out the basic outline of Sheldon's super asymmetry idea, for which they ultimately won the Nobel Prize in physics in the series' final episode.  Sheldon described his idea this way: "My equations have been trying to describe an imperfect world, and the only way to do that is to introduce imperfection into the underlying theory."

Of course, this was all fictional, but it illustrates something interesting regarding nonfictional reality.

In *Physical Review Letters*, Takashi Nishikawa and Adilson E. Motter wrote, "There are instances in which the observed behavior of the system can be symmetric only when the system itself is not. [We] called this effect asymmetry-induced symmetry, but could have referred to it as a form of super asymmetry since it epitomizes the notion that imperfections make things perfect."

Chaos theory, likewise, demonstrates that random imperfections can lead to order.

John Banzhaf, a physicist trained at MIT pointed out that the concept of super asymmetry indeed does have some relationship with reality and that we confront many asymmetries that we in fact rely upon.  The human body, for instance, is not perfectly symmetrical; our hearts are generally on the left side of our bodies.  The halves of our faces are not exactly alike; that's why people will comment, "this is my good side."  In fact, if one were to use Photoshop or similar graphics program and cut a face in half, reverse it, and then try combining it, the result will be a very weird looking face.  People usually part their hair asymmetrically because they think it looks more attractive that way.  Works of art and architecture also make use of asymmetries.  Banzhaf argues that the universe, in fact, is made up of asymmetries and other imperfections.  And such asymmetries are necessary for the universe to exist and function.  The implications of this are fascinating.

## Chapter Nine: The Actual Answer to the
## Actual Question

The short answer to the ultimate question of life, the universe and everything, is this: "In order for us to exist, imperfection is necessary."   And so the question, ultimately must *not* be "why do good people suffer if God is good and powerful," but *instead*, "is existence a good idea in the first place?"  Going back to the *Hitchhiker's Guide to the Galaxy*, or more specifically, one of its sequels, *The Restaurant at the End of the Universe*, we find these words:

> "The story so far:  In the beginning the Universe was created. This has made a lot of people very angry and been widely regarded as a bad move."

If the nature of existence requires imperfection, then "is existence a good idea?"  Despite the funny words in Douglas Adam's novel, most of us would probably answer in the affirmative. Especially given that imperfection is balanced, like any of the other forces of nature. Imperfection is moderate, rather than devastating, since devastating imperfection would lead to non-existence: it would destroy existence and render it impossible.

There was a *slight* imbalance between matter and antimatter following the Big Bang. If it had been perfectly balanced, nothing would exist. But too much one way or the other, and the universe would not have functioned in such a way as to allow life, any more than if gravity, the electro-weak, or the strong force, were not within a very narrow range.

The anthropic principle perhaps comes into play as we contemplate all of this.  The obvious realization is that the universe as it exists is obviously compatible with the existence of conscience, sapient life since we exist and are observing it.  John D. Barrow and Frank Tipler argued beyond this by saying that perhaps the principle in some way explains why this universe has the age and the fundamental physical constants necessary for conscious life to exist.  This is called the strong anthropic principle.  The critics of this point of view argue for what is called now the weak anthropic principle which argues that the universe's fine tuning is the result of "selection bias": only in a universe capable of supporting life will there be creatures capable of observing and reflecting on this fact and we just happened to have lucked out that everything came together just right for that to be the case.

In *The Salmon of Doubt: Hitchhiking the Galaxy One Last Time* (New York: Ballantine, pp. 131-132), published after his untimely death, Douglas Adams wrote:

> Imagine a puddle waking up one morning and thinking, "This is an interesting world I find myself in, an interesting hole I find myself in, fits me rather neatly, doesn't it? In fact it fits me staggeringly well, must have been made to have me in it!" This is such a powerful idea that as the sun rises in the sky and the air heats up and as, gradually, the puddle gets smaller and smaller, it's still frantically hanging on to the notion that everything's going to be alright, because this world was meant to have him in it, was built to have him in it; so the moment he disappears catches him rather by surprise. I think this may be something we need to be on the watch out for.

The puddle analogy, as this has subsequently been called, is a useful, if imperfect critique of the anthropic principle.  Jim Denny, in a blogpost on April 11, 2012 (*The Puzzle of Existence and a Puddle of Doubt, The Truth Will*

*Make You Mad*) wrote that as with all analogies, this one is imperfect, but he argues it is actually quite weak.   He points out:

> Adams begins: "Imagine a puddle waking up one morning and thinking..." He doesn't seem to realize that, in order for a puddle to wake up and think its first thought, a vast number of interconnected and incredibly unlikely coincidences have to occur.
>
> The Big Bang had to happen, and the Big Bang had to explode with just the right amount of force to allow matter to disperse evenly and smoothly and allow galaxies to form. Had the Big Bang not been precisely fine-tuned, our universe might consist of nothing but tenuous hydrogen gas—or a single supermassive black hole. The laws of nature had to be laid down at the instant of the Big Bang, and had to be fine-tuned to an accuracy of one part in the trillions before the universe itself could exist, much less a contemplative puddle.
>
> The electromagnetic force, the gravitational force, the strong nuclear force, and the weak nuclear force all had to be perfectly balanced in order for stars to form and begin cooking up the elements needed to make planets—silicon, nickel, iron, oxygen, magnesium, and so forth. Adams' pensive puddle could not find itself sitting in "an interesting hole" unless the hole was situated on a planet orbiting a star that was part of a galaxy that was created by the incredibly fine-tuned forces and conditions of the Big Bang.
>
> And in order for that puddle to wake up one morning and think at all, it would need to be a lot more complex than a mere puddle of water. A

thinking puddle would be a very complex puddle. Even if that puddle were comprised of exotic alien nerve cells suspended in a matrix of liquid ammonia, it would certainly need something like lipid molecules and protein structures and nucleic acids in order to become sufficiently evolved as to wake up and contemplate its own existence.

Such components require the existence of carbon. And if you know anything about where carbon comes from, you know that carbon doesn't grow on trees. It is formed in an amazingly fine-tuned process involving the precise placement of a nuclear resonance level in a beryllium atom. Any enlightened plashet would have to conclude that a superintellect had monkeyed with physics, chemistry, and the biological composition of pools and puddles.

The rest of Douglas Adams' scenario, in which "the sun rises in the sky and the air heats up and … the puddle gets smaller and smaller" is meaningless in view of the fact that dozens and dozens of events, forces, and conditions have to interact in a fine-tuned way in order for the sun to exist, the air to exist, the sky to exist, and the hole in the ground to exist, so that a puddle can wake up one morning and wonder about its place in the cosmic order.

The reason that the anthropic principle remains interesting and compelling is because of all the fine-tuning required for us to exist and be able to talk about the issue in the first place. And this principle has some impact then on our current discussion about the necessity of imperfection then for the universe to exist as it does; that is, imperfection seems to be a part of that necessary fine-tuning. And we see imperfection all over the place in our universe.

Oysters produce pearls because of an imperfection: a grain of dirt.

Planets follow ellipses, not perfect circles.

And even the Bible seems to agree with the universe being an imperfect place by God's design. God said things were *good*, not perfect at the creation. Genesis 1:31 summarizes what God was thinking at the end of the creative process:

> God saw all that he had made, and it was very good. And there was evening, and there was morning—the sixth day.

The preceding 30 verses before this commentary on the goodness of the world describe the creation of the universe, the earth, and all life on the planet, including the creation of human beings, both male and female, in the image of God. Chapter two, following that commentary, then goes into some added detail about the creation of humanity (already summarized in chapter one), a standard way that Semitic texts are often structured. That is, they are put together sort of like Russian nesting dolls, with the same story being repeated either from a different perspective, or in greater detail. Thus, in chapter one, the first verse is like the first paragraph of a newspaper article: it summarizes what the rest of the chapter is about. Genesis 1, verse 1 states that "In the beginning God created the heavens and the earth." From verse 2 through the end of the chapter, we get a more detailed picture of how God created the heavens and the earth, organized into six days. On the last day, God creates human beings.

In the expansion on the sixth day in chapter two God for the first time will say that something is "not good": in the more detailed description of the creation of people, when the man was alone, before the woman was created. God said that it was "not good" for the man to be alone.

And of course, the whole incident of God discovering something "not good" is covered, or included, in Genesis 1:31 when he says that everything is "good." The "not good" of the man being alone is part of the overall "good" of the created order once everything is finished—a finished creation that includes the serpent, the tree of the knowledge of good and evil that is prohibited to people, and the "not good," however temporary, of the man being alone.

The creation is considered good even though it had inherent flaws, even though it was not perfect. Voltaire quoted an Italian proverb in his *Dictionnaire philosophique* in 1770 that is commonly translated into English as "Perfect is the enemy of good." Aristotle argued for the principle of the golden mean which argues for balance in life and the avoidance of extremism. The author of Ecclesiastes seems to argue along the same way when he or she writes:

> In this meaningless life of mine I have seen both
> of these:
>
> the righteous perishing in their righteousness,
> and the wicked living long in their wickedness.
> Do not be overrighteous,
> neither be overwise—
> why destroy yourself?
> Do not be overwicked,
> and do not be a fool—
> why die before your time?
> It is good to grasp the one
> and not let go of the other.
> Whoever fears God will avoid all extremes.
> (Ecclesiastes 7:15-18)

The *Pareto Principle,* also known as the 80-20 rule, argues this concept numerically. It commonly takes 20 per cent of the full time to complete 80 per cent of a task, while to complete the last 20 per cent of a task takes 0 percent of the effort. Achieving absolute perfection may be impossible and so, as increasing effort results in diminishing returns, further activity becomes increasingly inefficient.

Robert Watson-Watt, the developer of the early warning radar in Great Britain used to counter the rapid growth of the Luftwaffe during World War II propounded a "cult of the imperfect." He is quoted as saying that "Give them the third best to go on with; the second best comes too late, the best never comes." The economist George Stigler argued that "If you never miss a plane, you're spending too much time at the airport."

A natural diamond crystal usually contains flaws. There are such things as flawless diamonds; they are called paragons, and they are exceptionally rare. Confucius is credited with saying that, "Better a diamond with a flaw, than a pebble without."

And so, from this "good" creation that God made, the Fall grew: the serpent seduced Eve, who seduced Adam, who then learned about good and evil, and who became subject to suffering and death—all for the "good" creation which God later in Genesis 6 "regrets" or "repents" of.

It will not be the last time that God "repents." One of the more interesting places is in the book of Job in its last chapter.

Job is described at the beginning of the book as being "perfect." It is emphasized that he is a righteous man and that he has done nothing wrong. Through the book Job maintains that he is innocent. And yet, horrible things happen to him. Why? Because Satan, at the beginning of the book, challenges God with the question: why does Job serve God? Isn't it because God has blessed him and made him prosperous? Therefore, if God makes life miserable for Job, if God takes everything away from Job, if God makes Job suffer in agony, then Job will curse God.

God does not agree with Satan's analysis of Job's attitude toward God, and so God lets Satan do his worst to him.  Meanwhile, Job's "friends" come to him and berate him.  They have the same point of view that Satan has: the only reason bad things are now happening to Job is because Job deserves them: he must have done something horrifically evil, or else he wouldn't have lost everything, even his health. Job, his friends warn him, needs to repent. Like Satan, they believe that good things come to those who behave well, and bad things come to those who don't. Any other belief would undermine piety.  Karma's a bitch, after all.

Job rejects the theology of his "friends" which is the theology of Satan.  And in the end, God criticizes Job's so-called friends and informs them that all their arguments were wrong, while everything Job said was right.

One of the more intriguing parts of the whole episode comes near the end, in Job 42:1-7 which is usually translated this way:

> Then Job replied to the LORD:
> "I know that you can do all things;
> no purpose of yours can be thwarted.
> You asked, 'Who is this that obscures my plans
> without knowledge?'
> Surely I spoke of things I did not understand,
> things too wonderful for me to know.
> "You said, 'Listen now, and I will speak;
> I will question you,
> and you shall answer me.'
> My ears had heard of you
> but now my eyes have seen you.
> Therefore I despise myself
> and repent in dust and ashes."

After the LORD had said these things to Job, he said to Eliphaz the Temanite, "I am angry with you and your two friends, because you have not spoken the truth about me, as my servant Job has.

Which has Job despising himself and repenting in dust and ashes.

There is a problem with this traditional way of understanding the passage however, because the beginning of verse seven then makes no sense, since it says "After the Lord had said these things to Job" but the preceding words are being understood as having been spoken not by God, but by Job.  So what's going on?

The quotation marks are in the wrong place, and a couple of words, added by the translators not in the actual Hebrew text need to be eliminated.  Once that is done, the passage works, and leads us to a transformative understanding of God and the world.

Verses 1 through 3 are fine as they are:

Then Job replied to the LORD:

"I know that you can do all things;
no purpose of yours can be thwarted.
You asked, 'Who is this that obscures my plans without knowledge?'
Surely I spoke of things I did not understand,
things too wonderful for me to know.

Verse four is where things need to be altered.  "You said" is not there in Hebrew.  Rather, Job now addresses God and demands that, now that God has had his say, he needs to respond to Job—which is something that Job has been asking for throughout the book: "I want to confront God, I want to ask him what's up, why is this happening to me.  Prove my guilt."

And so Job says to God:

"Listen now, and I will speak;
I will question you,
and you shall answer me."

And then, verses 5 and 6 are not Job's words at all. They are God's words in response to Job:

"My ears had heard of you
but now my eyes have seen you.
Therefore I despise myself
and repent in dust and ashes."

God relents and acknowledges that Job has suffered unjustly, for no reason, as God himself had told Satan back at the beginning of the story in Job 2:3. And God uses a formula common in a legal setting to acknowledge Job's ignorance, and then, in what follows, God berates Job's friends, and, in tune with the legal requirements we find in the Mosaic legislation (for example Exodus 22:4), God pays back Job double for what he has been deprived of. He lives 140 years, double the normal "three score and ten" allotted to human beings, making up for his illness, he receives double of his lost wealth, and he receives double of his lost children. The last might, on the face of it, seem insufficient, but in Jewish thinking (and in that of this era of history), the loss of children was not on the same level as say the loss of parents: one would mourn double the length of time for parents who died as for children who died, because parents could not be replaces, while children, realistically, could be. And it should be noted that prior to the advent of good antibiotics and other medical treatment in the twentieth century, on average one in four children succumbed to childhood illnesses before the age of five. Likewise, women commonly died during for due to complications from childbirth.  My own mother's mother died from complications with childbirth in 1932—from issues not at all life-threatening and easily treatable today.

God "repents" of what happened to Job.  The Hebrew word used there is *naham*, which means "to repent, to be sorry for, to suffer grief as a result of what one has done." This is something God does not infrequently in the Bible. Generally, interpreters find ways of, to put it bluntly, explain it away, rather than considering the implications and what it may tell us about God and the nature of the universe.

A good day at Disneyland has been had even if you have a slight sunburn.  It becomes a bad day only if you have heatstroke and third-degree burns.  A slight imperfection is still good. Imperfection does not preclude something being good.  Imperfection does not mean bad.

We are, as Carl Sagan so eloquently put it, star stuff. We are made of the imperfection of the universe, and so we exist as likewise imperfect, but it is balanced just right: anymore and it would be too much, any less and it wouldn't exist at all.  Suffering of a certain level, but not more than a certain level, is an inevitable result of our existing at all.

Philosophers have looked at the universe and commented that we can imagine a universe with less suffering, just a little less; so why, if God exists, do we not have that sort of universe.  I suspect that the answer is similar to what we get with the anthropic principle: the basic forces of the universe are three (or 4, depending on how you divide them and physics would like to get it all down to one); they are gravity, electro-magnetism, weak force, and the strong force.  Electro-magnetism and the weak force seem to be related and are sometimes labeled the electro-weak force.  Gravity is a consequence of mass; it is the weakest of the forces. Electro-magnetism is very strong: electricity and magnates are obvious examples from everyday life; the weak force we see at the subatomic level and it is responsible for nuclear decay: that is, for instance, carbon14 decaying into stable carbon 12, or uranium decaying eventually into lead; the strong force is the most powerful, but it operates only over incredibly short distances: it is what holds the nucleus of an atom together. Where all this gets especially interesting is in the interaction of these forces with one another and the level of strength in relationship with one another. That is, if say the strong force were slightly less strong, or the force of gravity was slightly stronger, or slightly less strong, one winds up with universes that would never produce life: that is, stars would go through their life cycles too quickly, or they might not form at all, and so on. Only when the various forces are precisely balanced as they are in our universe, do we have a universe that works this way, where life can exist. It is easy to imagine the forces having different values than they do; and we guess that the values were established at the moment of the Big Bang, but we do not know why they are the way they are: that is, we do not know of any laws of physics that preclude them from being other than they are.

Likewise, at the beginning, the amount of matter and anti-matter in the universe should have been equal, but wasn't; there was slightly more matter than antimatter, and so when the inevitable annihilations occurred, matter wound up being dominant; the slight imperfection meant a universe with stuff in it as opposed to an empty universe with nothing, the presumed state of things prior to the existence of the universe. Of course, thinking of "before" is not quite right, since time didn't exist until the universe came to exist.

Thinking of all this in this rather abstract, theoretical way is easier to handle then when we start including the actual imperfections of the world; suffering is not theoretical and it is not abstract when you are the one suffering. When you are being shoved into a Nazi "shower" that will kill you with poison gas, when your child is dying of leukemia, when your father was murdered by the Khmer Rouge, when communists starved your village in the Ukraine and imprisoned you in the Gulag—that's an imperfection that seems awfully big and bad.

But what we call the imperfections in the universe as a whole seem rather big from our perspective, after all.  The imperfections rendering a slight imbalance between matter and energy leave us with enormous galaxies, stars, and our rather substantial planet upon which we live and breathe and die, upon which all of the human story has been played out.  We are, after all, made of the very star stuff , the imperfect leftovers of our necessarily imbalanced universe; we live due to our ability to consume other life, to use the second law of thermodynamics—entropy—to our advantage, to fight against the otherwise inevitable evening, and the ultimate elimination of all imperfection or asymmetry.

Imperfection is what has made life possible at all. It is the asymmetry of reality that means we are, but that also means that our lives are also asymmetrical, inevitably: suffering is endemic of existence at all.  We cannot escape it if we would exist.

If we want to eliminate suffering, we would never then exist.  A more balanced universe would preclude existence, and thereby preclude suffering.

So. Is non-existing then preferable to existing?

God would answer "no," and so we exist.

Not all would agree with God, of course.  We still have the comic, tongue-in-cheek comment from *The Restaurant at the End of the Universe* by Douglas Adams mentioned before:

> "The story so far:
> In the beginning the Universe was created.

This has made a lot of people very angry and
been widely regarded as a bad move."

Unsurprisingly, there are thinkers who completely
agree with Adams. Opposition to the existence of sentience
is actually a serious philosophical position. It is called
antinatalism. Those who hold this point of view honestly
believe it would have been better had we never been born.
In a sense, they have taken the words of the author of
Ecclesiastes and built a philosophy with it:

Again I looked and saw all the oppression that was
taking place under the sun:

I saw the tears of the oppressed—
and they have no comforter;
power was on the side of their oppressors—
and they have no comforter.
And I declared that the dead,
who had already died,
are happier than the living,
who are still alive.
But better than both
is the one who has never been born,
who has not seen the evil
that is done under the sun. (Ecclesiastes 4:1-3)

Job personalized it:

After this, Job opened his mouth and cursed the day of
his birth. He said:

"May the day of my birth perish,
and the night that said, 'A boy is conceived!'
That day—may it turn to darkness;
may God above not care about it;
may no light shine on it.
May gloom and utter darkness claim it once more;

may a cloud settle over it;
may blackness overwhelm it.
That night—may thick darkness seize it;
may it not be included among the days of the year
nor be entered in any of the months.
May that night be barren;
may no shout of joy be heard in it.
May those who curse days curse that day,
those who are ready to rouse Leviathan.
May its morning stars become dark;
may it wait for daylight in vain
and not see the first rays of dawn,
for it did not shut the doors of the womb on me
to hide trouble from my eyes.

"Why did I not perish at birth,
and die as I came from the womb?
Why were there knees to receive me
and breasts that I might be nursed?
For now I would be lying down in peace;
I would be asleep and at rest
with kings and rulers of the earth,
who built for themselves places now lying in ruins,
with princes who had gold,
who filled their houses with silver.
Or why was I not hidden away in the ground like a
     stillborn child,
like an infant who never saw the light of day?
There the wicked cease from turmoil,
and there the weary are at rest.
Captives also enjoy their ease;
they no longer hear the slave driver's shout.
The small and the great are there,
and the slaves are freed from their owners.

"Why is light given to those in misery,
and life to the bitter of soul,

to those who long for death that does not come,
who search for it more than for hidden treasure,
who are filled with gladness
and rejoice when they reach the grave?
Why is life given to a man
whose way is hidden,
whom God has hedged in?
For sighing has become my daily food;
my groans pour out like water.
What I feared has come upon me;
what I dreaded has happened to me.
I have no peace, no quietness;
I have no rest, but only turmoil." (Job 3:1-26)

So, antinatalism, joining the author of Ecclesiastes, Job, and the comment by Douglas Adams regarding the questionable wisdom of creation argues that the presence of suffering in the world means that existence should never have happened. Existence, because of suffering, is by definition evil. If suffering was an unavoidable part of existence, then if there had been a God, the inevitability of suffering should have made him decide existence wasn't worth it. Better not to have ever been than to get sick, to feel pain and loss, and finally to die. Our very existence, according to antinatalists, is a great evil unworthy of the Creator.

Antinatilism embraces negative utilitarianism: that minimizing suffering has greater moral importance than maximizing happiness. Therefore, it is immoral to procreate. It is better to never have been, than to bring a person into the world, a person who will inevitably suffer and then die. Why cause suffering and death by permitting the birth of more humans? Every baby born is a tragedy.

David Benatar (born 1966) is a South African philosopher, academic and author. He received his PhD from the University of Cape Town and is best known for his advocacy of antinatalism in his book *Better Never to Have Been: The Harm of Coming into Existence* (Oxford University Press, 2006).

He argues, number one, that coming into existence is always a serious harm. Number two, he asserts that it is always wrong to have children. Number three, he believes it is wrong *not* to abort fetuses at the earlier stages of gestation. And number four, he insists it would be better if, as a result of there being no new people, humanity became extinct.

He thinks that there is a crucial asymmetry between pleasure and pain:

- the presence of pain is bad
- the presence of pleasure is good
- the absence of pain is good, even if that good is not enjoyed by anyone
- the absence of pleasure is not bad unless there is somebody for whom this absence is a deprivation

Therefore, according to antinatilists, the best possible world is one that lacks anyone in it able to experience pain. The world can be good only when people cease to exist.

One can understand and follow the logic of antinatlism quite easily and in many ways, it is a seductive point of view. But Ecclesiastes 7:13-14 exclaims:

Consider what God has done:
Who can straighten
what he has made crooked?
When times are good, be happy;
but when times are bad, consider this:
God has made the one
as well as the other.
Therefore, no one can discover

anything about their future.

The problem with antinatalism is with its basic premise.

Why is minimalizing moral suffering the guiding principle?

Why is *that* the most important thing?

Why do we *feel* that is important?

There are unexamined presuppositions mixed up in antinatalism. Obviously, we don't like the experience of being kicked in the groin. But we do enjoy the experience orgasms. The contrast between those two possibilities seems an overly subjective reason for arguing that humanity would be better off extinct than to ever suffer any unhappiness or pain ever.

What makes pain necessarily unmitigated evil? What is the basis for that moral judgment?

Antinatalism takes the argument of Voltaire and like-thinking atheists to its logical conclusion: not only should God not exist, humanity should not exist. And in fact, no sentient being under any circumstances out to exist. Creation, existence itself, was a mistake.

Given that we do exist, however, I think the argument is fundamentally flawed.

It takes the avoidance of pain and maximizes it. By taking it to its logical extreme, it demonstrates that the whole point of view is ultimately absurd and ludicrous.

Voltair's argument, and the argument of all those who ask the question, why do bad things happen to good people if God is good, loving and all powerful, presupposes the logic of antinatilism. I saw a meme on Facebook that showed a photograph with the words "There is no problem too big that God cannot solve." That was followed by a picture of starving children and the statement "I dare you to explain this without insulting my intelligence." That is, a demand to reconcile the first statement about God with the reality of the suffering depicted.

The problem with that meme, and the argument inherent in it, is that the person who set it up *doesn't want an answer*. He or she doesn't believe there *is* an answer. In fact, he or she wants you to shut up because he knows you're wrong and stupid. The question, ultimately, is not rational at all. It is entirely raw emotion.

It isn't even the right question.

And the problem of course is that besides asking the wrong question—remember my discussion about 42—it is, in point of fact, a strawman argument.

What's a strawman argument? Imagine a politician standing up and stating "My opponent believes that African Americans should be returned to slavery. Slavery is evil. How could my opponent believe such a thing? My opponent is wrong and evil. Are you evil? Do you want to be associated with that evil? Then don't vote for him."

Sounds awful. Everyone agrees slavery is evil. But if one's opponent doesn't actually believe what you claim he believes, you haven't actually given a real argument to oppose voting for your opponent.

A strawman argument is making up what someone believes, attributing it to them, and then tearing that "strawman" you've constructed to pieces. But your accusation isn't what your opponent believes. You've attributed something bad to him, and then you demolish that bad thing. Which has nothing to do with your opponent at all.

The Bible reveals that God is at work in the world, but never like a fairy godmother. God never denies the existence of suffering and evil. He never promises that his people will be spared suffering and evil. Quite the opposite.

But some people believe that God should make such a promise. That such a fairy-tale God is the one that everyone believes in, and that such a fairy-tale God is obviously at odds with reality, so the fairy-tale God is nonsense on stilts. It explains the issue that so troubles some people, especially in the modern era (post Voltaire): if God is good, then why is there suffering? The answer is simple: because the world is full of people who are free to mostly do whatever the hell they want, in a universe where "time and chance happen to all." (Ecclesiastes 9:11). The assumption that God is a genie who will snap his fingers and make all the world's troubles vanish is simply a fairy tale. Instead, God works gradually and intermittently, in ways that sometimes seem less than satisfying, because existence is necessarily asymmetrical: imperfect. Otherwise, there would be no existence.

The problem with the God of Big Rock Candy Mountain argument—it is the same one Voltaire came up with in *Candide*—is that it is a strawman argument. It argues that God is a magic fairy who sprinkles magic fairy dust and makes everything beautiful. But since we see no magic fairy dust and everything is not beautiful, then he must not exist or doesn't care. And as far as it goes, that is obviously the case. The God of Big Rock Candy Mountain doesn't exist. But his non-existence has nothing to do with the God of the Real Mountain.

Reality is something else. We do not—or at least should not—believe in a magic fairy God. The Bible does not paint a world that is anything other than filled with pain. When Elijah was alive, there were many suffering people. But he solved the problems of only a handful—and then only some of their problems, not all of them. As Jesus himself pointed out:

> "I assure you that there were many widows in
> Israel in Elijah's time, when the sky was shut for
> three and a half years and there was a severe
> famine throughout the land. Yet Elijah was not

sent to any of them, but to a widow in Zarephath in the region of Sidon. And there were many in Israel with leprosy in the time of Elisha the prophet, yet not one of them was cleansed—only Naaman the Syrian." (Luke 4:24-27)

When Jesus walked the planet, he healed some people. He raised a few dead ones back to life. But most people in the world stayed sick, most people in Israel stayed sick, and most of the dead people stayed in the ground. Those who stayed dead were no worse sinners than those who ended up being raised to life. He didn't help anyone win a lottery. He didn't make the poor widow who gave all she had into a rich woman (Luke 21:1-4). He merely made note of her sacrifice. But she stayed poor, as far as we know.

The Bible does not paint a world any different than the world in which we live today. It tells us of the handful of unusual circumstances that happened to a few people here and there over thousands of years. Most people never saw a miracle, most never got face time with God, and most never even heard the preaching of a prophet.

Our God is the God who rescued the Israelites from slavery. But he's also the God who let generations of Israelites be born in slavery, live in slavery, and die in slavery. God does not work quickly in the Bible, even when his hand is obvious. He allows people to do bad things for a long time. Tyrants remain tyrannical. They cause suffering for a long time. John the Baptist got beheaded for his trouble. Stephen got stoned to death. The prophet Isaiah was sawn in half by King Manasseh. God directs, redirects, and after the passage of years or even generations, he occasionally, and temporarily, ends the pain. But there are never any guarantees beyond the words of Jesus: "in this world you will have trouble."

After four hundred years of the Israelites living as oppressed slaves, he sent Moses to Egypt; ten plagues over many months or years followed.  And eventually, Pharaoh agreed to let the people go.  God did not simply transport them out of their slavery using a Star Trek style transporter.  Nor did he kill off all the Egyptians with a rain of fire and brimstone.

Our God is not a magic fairy God.  He does not promise us that he will fix all our problems.  Jesus, in fact, promised us persecution.  From the beginning, we witness murder and destruction.  Jesus describes persecution from one end of scripture to the other: "the blood of righteous Abel to the blood of Zechariah son of Berekiah, whom you murdered between the temple and the altar." (Mt 23:35) Today throughout the world Christians are being rounded up and slaughtered.  Our God is not a magic fairy God, the God skeptics abhor.  Our God is the God who came and became one of us, lived with us, bled for us, died for us and saved us from our sins.  Our God is a God who himself suffered.

Our God is a God who may let us die gruesomely, he may let our baby die from SIDS; he may let us lose our house, he may let our car get repossessed.  He may let us get sick and never get well.  He may let us, or a loved one, or a child or a spouse suffer from serious mental illness.  He *will* let us all die sooner or later, every last one of us, no matter how much we exercise or eat right.  That is the God we worship, not this make-believe fairy God of the magic fairy dust.

He told us he would be with us through it all; that it would perhaps be awful and hard; but he would stay at our side.  The Lutheran pastor Dietrich Bonhoeffer died naked, hanged by the Nazis with piano wire, just two weeks before Germany surrendered.  God did not save him from that awful fate; his rescue came two weeks too late for him.  In the New Testament, the author of the book of Hebrews writes:

"Some faced jeers and flogging,□□ and even chains and imprisonment.□□ They were put to death by stoning;□□□□ they were sawed in two; they were killed by the sword.□□ They went about in sheepskins and goatskins,□□ destitute, persecuted and mistreated— the world was not worthy of them. They wandered in deserts and mountains, and in caves□□ and holes in the ground.

"These were all commended□□ for their faith, yet none of them received what had been promised.□□ God had planned something better for us so that only together with us□□ would they be made perfect.□□" (Hebrews 11:36-40)

That is the God we worship, that is the God we trust, that is the God who exists.  Our God is the God who promised to be with us until the end of the world, the God whose suffering we would participate in, not the God who would keep us from pain:

I want to know Christ—yes, to know the power of his resurrection and participation in his sufferings, becoming like him in his death (Philippians 3:10)

And,

To this you were called, because Christ suffered for you, leaving you an example, that you should follow in his steps. (1 Peter 2:21)

And,

Dear friends, do not be surprised at the fiery ordeal that has come on you to test you, as though something strange were happening to you. (1 Peter 4:12)

And,

Do not be surprised, my brothers and sisters, if the world hates you. (1 John 3:13)

This is our God. Not a magic fairy.

Of the twelve apostles, Jesus' closest companions, witnesses to his resurrection, all but one was martyred. The one who wasn't, John, according to tradition, was boiled in oil but survived, and was exiled to a small island called Patmos. His life was not sprinkled by much fairy dust, either. And he still died eventually, just like the rest of us will. One way or another.

But life is not just suffering, either. There are good times in life. In fact, mostly good times: graduations and weddings, babies and springtime. The captives are set free; the prisoner of war comes home. The trapped miners are rescued, the lost campers are found, the missing child comes back, the prodigal returns home. The sick are healed, the blind see, and the dead come back to life. There are times of celebration, and great joy; there are new jobs, and new contracts, there are successes and winners. The drought ends. The fires are quenched. The mountain moves and drops into the sea. Life sometimes is so good you can't believe it. Sometimes you prosper.

Life is both. Life is neither.

As Solomon wrote, if times are good rejoice; if not, remember: both come from God. Our God is all those things. Our God is real, not rainbows and unicorns.

* * *

The essence of existentialism is that *you* are the measure: you are the one who makes your own reality, who makes your own meaning in life, your own purpose.  It's all about how you feel.

And so they create God after their own likeness, according to their own image. Polytheism is great for that. It is the ADHD of theology.  Can't make up your mind? Just keep looking; sooner or later maybe you'll find a deity that matches your purpose, that satisfies your longing, that lives up to what you want to find in a god.  You don't like pizza?  Maybe you'll like sushi.  You don't like green salsa; maybe red will be your speed.  Not a hamburger person?  Maybe pulled pork sandwiches!

Is God just whatever we want him to be?  I once stood in front of a class of students and asked for a for volunteers to "Give me the name of your favorite song."

I carefully wrote their choices up on a whiteboard. Then, after a dozen or so had done that, I held up a glass jar a filled with jellybeans and asked, "How many beans would you guess are in this jar of jellybeans?"

And then I wrote the guesses down on the board as well.

Finally, I asked one of the students who had given me her favorite song title, "What if I told you you're wrong for liking that song?"

Her eyes went big.

"Would you like that? What would you think of me for saying that?  You'd think I was a jerk. You'd say I was stupid.  Who am I to tell you what song you like or don't like?"

She nodded.

"But what if I told you that you'd guessed wrong about the number of beans in the jar?  Would you be mad? Would you call me a jerk?"

She shook her head.

"Why?"

"Because there are a specific number of jellybeans in the jar."

So.

Tell me: Is God more like a list of favorite songs—or is God more akin to a jar of jellybeans?

Wait, wait—let's make this easier.

Is your best friend more like a list of songs, or a jar of jellybeans?

Then the answer to the question is obvious. Your friend is like a jar of jellybeans.

Why? Because there is an answer to how many jellybeans are in this jar. A specific answer. One answer. You can make a lot of guesses, but only one number can be right, while an infinite number can be wrong. You can make specific truth claims about the jar of jellybeans: weight, size, colors of the beans, and the numbers.

Your friend's attributes are not subjective. His height, his weight, his political preferences and favorite song are not meaningful and real only as I determine. His reality is not dependent upon my *feelings* about what his character traits and personality might be like. Your friend is objectively there, objectively in possession of certain qualities regardless of me or my feelings. His reality or lack thereof has nothing to do with how I conceive of him, what I want to imagine about him. What he is—well, that's what he is: blond, blue-eyed, or whatever.

If I conceive of my wife as good at picking up after herself, but she in fact leaves piles all over the house, why am I surprised? Does it mean that my wife doesn't exist? If you conceive of your husband as a good cook, but he doesn't even know how to turn on the stove, does that mean he will cook you dinner tonight and it will turn out well? How disappointed will you be? If my wife conceives that I have a good sense of direction and she lets me drive and we head off to Disneyland, how disappointed will she be when we end up in Milwaukee?

People lose faith in God, get disappointed by God, get mad at God because he doesn't live up to their expectations of who he is.  People are regularly devastated by what they perceive as God's failures.

But it wasn't *God* who failed.  It was their *conception* of God who failed.

When I failed to get us to Disneyland, my wife's conception of me as a map, and her thereby giving me the wheel of the car, is the true source of her disappointment and our failure.

The Real God cannot fail you; only the God of your imagination can do that.  If you don't know God as he is, then your mistaken expectations of him will let you down all the time.

The disciples were often confused by Jesus; it was not Jesus' fault.  He wasn't being confusing. It's just that the disciples had certain…expectations.  Jesus said "I am the messiah" and so they knew what that meant: he was the king, he'd kick out the Romans, he'd rule the world and they'd be on the ground floor.  Jesus said "I'm going to Jerusalem and there I'll be crucified and die, buried, and rise again in three days."  The disciples were confused. That didn't fit the conception. Didn't fit the narrative.

In John 14 we see Jesus tell his disciples "Peace I leave with you; my peace I give you.  I do not give to you as the world gives.  Do not let your hearts be troubled and do not be afraid. (14:27) And then he says "I have told you this so that my joy may be in you and that your joy may be complete." (John 15:11); and "And I will do whatever you ask in my name, so that the Father may be glorified in the Son.  You may ask me for anything in my name, and I will do it." (14:13)

But he also said, "If the world hates you, keep in mind that it hated me first. If you belonged to the world, it would love you as its own. As it is, you do not belong to the world, but I have chosen you out of the world. That is why the world hates you. Remember what I told you: 'A servant is not greater than his master.' If they persecuted me, they will persecute you also." (John 15:18-20)

He went on: "All this I have told you so that you will not fall away. They will put you out of the synagogue; in fact, the time is coming when anyone who kills you will think they are offering a service to God. They will do such things because they have not known the Father or me. I have told you this, so that when their time comes you will remember." (John 16:1-4)

But we still become confused. Because we have expectations. Because we want the one and not the other. We want to get anything we ask for. We want peace. This stuff about persecution and getting killed, not so much do we want that.

But God is real. And he is what he is. Not what we wish. Not what we make of it ourselves, as per existentialism. Not the magic fairy god. We get confused because we don't want to face reality. We *like* the fantasy, and so we go "la-la-la" and try to drown out what doesn't fit inside the picture we painted. "I reject your reality and substitute my own," as one of the Mythbusters said with tongue firmly in cheek.

So how's that working out for you?

"I have told you these things, [Jesus said] so that in me you may have peace. In this world you will have trouble. But take heart! I have overcome the world." (John 16:33)

About any human being, we can say a whole lot of things that are false. If I say you're ugly when you've just been crowned Miss Universe, or if I say you're a man when you're obviously a woman, then I'm wrong. Your height is what it is, along with your weight, your hair color, your eye color, your skin tone, the number of teeth in your mouth, your politics, your marital status, and your fondness or not for broccoli. These statistics are what they are, regardless of what I might say about them.

When it comes to talking about God, it works the same way. He is not a matter of our opinion or preferences. Does he have a hankering for brussels sprouts? Does he hate the Chicago Cubs? There are answers to those questions.

If God exists, then he is what he is, not what you imagine him to be, not what you make of him. If he is not real in the same way that your wife is real, or the sandwich you had for lunch, then he doesn't exist at all. God is not what you hope he is. God is not what you want him to be. God is himself. His own essence.

If you say your friend over there is a pile of steaming dog poop, and an awful human being, well, that thought, that "meaning" you've created is, well—what is actually a steaming pile of dog poop if your friend is actually a wonderful human being.

God is as real as you are. And you are who you are, regardless of what someone thinks of you. God is who he is, regardless of what I want to imagine of him.

The author of Ecclesiastes wrote that God made people upright, but they've gone in search of many schemes. We make crap up. We think we can create God in our image, make him be what we'd like him to be. And so we create a strawman that fails us at the first sign of trouble.

You want to be able to survive the storms of life, to make sense of your life, to live your life? Then you need to find out who God is. And then accept that he is who he is regardless of what you'd rather imagine. Wisdom is to recognize reality and accept it. God is real. As real as you. As real as me. You are this way, and not that way. God is this way and not that way.

Accept God as he is. That's who will save you. That's who will be with you. That's who will see you through life with all its ups and downs. Ups are easy. Downs aren't. Downs are when you need the real God, not the strawman you built like a list of song titles. That list won't comfort you when your favorite person perishes.

The author of Hebrews wrote,

> And without faith it is impossible to please God, because anyone who comes to him must believe that he exists and that he rewards those who earnestly seek him. (Hebrews 11:6)

We do not put our faith in faith. We do not put our faith in the magic fairy god. We do not, cannot put much faith in the God as we conceive of him, the God who exists as we grant him meaning. God cannot be simply the Santa Claus of Francis Church, who answered Virginia O'Hanlon in an editorial of the *New York Sun* on September 21, 1897 that "Yes, Virginia, there is a Santa Clause" as long as there is love and kindness and the joy of Christmas. If God for you is like Santa Claus for that editor of the *New York Sun*, then you don't believe in God; you believe in wishful thinking. If God is not as real as you and I, then he doesn't exist. If we pray to that sort of God—one of our own making—if we depend on that God in times of trouble, then woe to us, we are of all people most miserable. We must know and put our faith in the God who is, the God who exists.

Cling to the real God. *That's* the wisdom that will brighten your face, that will change its hard appearance.

The atheists are right. We all agree they are. In fact, every last one of us is an atheist, too. Do you believe in Zeus? How about Molech? Marduk? Poseidon? Ares? Astoreth? The earliest Christians were condemned as atheists.

The God of today's atheists, however, is a strawman God. That God they say does not exist, well, he does not exist and you agree with them that he does not exist. Or you should.

If you believe that God wants you to be rich, healthy, and prosperous, than you are believing in the God of the atheists. And you are an idiot. The fool has said in his heart that there is no God. But the fool also says that the stick of wood he's bowing to is God. Either one is a moron. The God promising us rose gardens is not the God who exists. You're going to die and end up in a hole in the ground. You are not going to be rich. You are not going to be healthy. You are going to be dead. Dead in a hole in the ground.

If you don't believe in the God who will let you end up dead in a hole in the ground, then you are a fool. Because atheists reject a God that wants you to be healthy and wealthy. They can prove to you that such a God doesn't exist and they are absolutely, without a doubt right. As right as you are to reject Molech, Thor, and Zeus.

Reality does not often fit our fantasy, our hopes, our desires—what we really want. And so we come full circle.

There is the world that we wish for and then there is the world that is. We would do well to develop our theology to match the world that is, rather than the ideal we wish could be.

Ecclesiastes is a hard book. A harsh book. A bucket of cold water in the face book. It pries our eyes open and forces us to stare unblinking at the harsh light of the world we actually live in.

The part of it here, now, around us—"under the sun" as he puts it. Cut off from God. See, the reality also includes this: God has hidden himself. He makes himself hard to see…unless we are looking for him; unless we expect him to be there. Unless we "listen to the still small voice" that the prophet Elijah heard. God can always be explained away. The skeptic can never be convinced of God's involvement in your life; he may politely listen to you and mouth platitudes, but in his heart of hearts, he knows that there are other ways of explaining your experience that he believes you're just refusing to face.

## Chapter Ten: So

The seventeenth century philosopher and theologian Gottfried Leibniz argued that if God is good, loving, and powerful, then this must be the best possible world, because what other kind of world would such a deity create?

The problem, of course, is that we can imagine a better world.  One of the common clichés people mutter at us in our times of grief when a loved one passes on is, "well, she's in a better place now."

So, if there is such a better place, such a better world, then why is there this one and why do we have to be in it, if God loves us so much?

If the Kingdom of Heaven is better than here and now, then how can this possibly be the best of all possible worlds?  And if this isn't the best of all possible worlds, then what does that tell us about God?

But.

What if the Kingdom of Heaven can come about only because of this world?  That is, what if the Kingdom of Heaven *requires* this world in order to come into existence?  What if, in fact, this world creates the Kingdom of Heaven, so that the Kingdom of Heaven is a consequence of this world?

The Kingdom of Heaven would then grow from this world and would not entirely—or even at all—be separate from this world.

Some may object to this for various reasons, but ask yourself this fundamental question: what is the Kingdom of Heaven?

The short answer: it is God's people.  It is the church.  It is the Bride of Christ.

Therefore, this world is necessary for the Kingdom of Heaven to exist, because it is the people of God living in this world who are and who become that Kingdom. This then is the best of all possible worlds, since it is the only world that can create or become the better world of the Kingdom—which is paradoxical unless you realize that the Kingdom is co-existent with this current world: the Kingdom, in a very real sense, is now.

Jesus explained it very clearly:

Once, having been asked by the Pharisees when the kingdom of God would come, Jesus replied, "The kingdom of God does not come with your careful observation, nor will people say, 'Here it is,' or 'There it is,' because the kingdom of God is within you." (Luke 17:20-21)

When we ask, "is this the best of all possible worlds?" we must recognize that this world includes the Kingdom of Heaven in seed form at the very least.

Ask yourself this when you peer at Jesus sleeping in the manger, "is this baby the best of all possible human beings?" The baby is no less the Son of God, the Messiah, the Savior of the World, than the resurrected Lord. One could say that this world is the baby to the adult that is the Kingdom of Heaven.

An analogy from scripture would be Joseph. After the death of his father Jacob, his brothers were fearful, scared to death, that Joseph would seek vengeance against them for all the awful things they'd done to him, like selling him into slavery, and for all the awful things he'd gone through after that. So what happened?

But Joseph said to them, "Don't be afraid. Am I in the place of God? You intended to harm me, but God intended it for good to accomplish what is now being done, the saving of many lives. So then, don't be afraid. I will provide for you and your children." And he reassured them and spoke kindly to them. (Genesis 51:19-21)

Consider, too, that even the death of the righteous—what most would consider an example of the core problem in the issue of suffering being unjust and an affront to the existence of God—is, counterintuitively, considered to be a positive good, a blessing even, based on a few biblical passages.  As I've pointed out before, it is death that makes our redemption possible in the first place. Our exclusion from the tree of life, God's concern that we not be allowed to eat from it and "live forever" (see Genesis 3:21-24), was not done because he hated us, because he was mad at us, because he wanted to make us squirm; it was because our being mortal was the only way he could save us: God had to become a human being, become one of us, and then die for our sins.  If human beings were not mortal, he could not die for us and if he could not die for us…then we could not be saved.  This is why Satan and the demons are doomed: they are immortal and beyond help or hope.

We die because God loves us; and love is the core of the Bible, the center of everything, as we see for instance in Matthew 22:36-40:

> "Teacher, which is the greatest commandment in the Law?"
> Jesus replied: " 'Love the Lord your God with all your heart and with all your soul and with all your mind.' This is the first and greatest commandment. And the second is like it: 'Love your neighbor as yourself.'  All the Law and the Prophets hang on these two commandments."

Love is the core of the Bible. Jesus pointed out that it was on the twin commandments, to love God and to love people, that the whole Bible hung. Paul emphasizes it in his writing, too. He explained that all the commandments in the Bible could be summarized with a single commandment: "love your neighbor as yourself" (Romans 13:9 and Galatians 5:14). This concept is also a core concept in Judaism. The story is told of a gentile wishing to convert to Judaism. Finding the Rabbi Hillel, he asked him to recite the entire Torah while standing on one foot. The rabbi's response was to say "Love the Lord your God with all your heart, mind and soul and love your neighbor as yourself. All the rest is commentary."

Because of love, Christians should be the most optimistic of people.

The way of the world is to be gloomy, to always expect the worst, to believe that ultimately there is no hope. The world embraces pessimism.

The reason we keep going in the face of problems, in the face of setbacks, in the face of discouragement and nothing going right is precisely because of this thing called love. We keep our zeal, our spiritual fervor, we keep on serving the Lord because we know God loves us. And his love inspires us to love the people around us, and to press on.

Think about how a young man or woman feel in the first throws of love. Nothing else matters. Everything is beautiful and all is right with the world. Nothing else matters as long as he or she is loved and loves in return.

*That's* what our relationship with God can do for us. *That's* the power of true love.

What did Paul write about grief, about how we react when someone dies? Not that we aren't sad, but that we "do not grieve like the rest of mankind, who have no hope" (1 Thessalonians 4:13). Why? Because we know God loves us we can face the worst without despair.

We understand that things will work out for our good. As Paul wrote,

"I am convinced that neither death nor life, neither angels nor demons, neither the present nor the future, nor any powers, neither height nor depth, nor anything else in all creation, will be able to separate us from the love of God that is in Christ Jesus our Lord." (Romans 8:38-39)

What does suffering tell us about God? Counterintuitively: God loves us. Why? Because, like our friends when we grieve, he is right there with us. He not only suffered on the cross for us, he also suffers with us as we suffer. And he never leaves us nor forsakes us. Like our loved ones, our friends, our family, God loves us and he is right there with us, grieving with us. He may say nothing. We may not feel him. But he is there. Because he loves us.

## Chapter Eleven: The End of the Matter

We really are unrighteous, all of us.  So shouldn't we all suffer all the time?  That's been prosed as an explanation for why people suffer.  No one is righteous, Paul said, quoting from various places in the Old Testament:

As it is written:

"There is no one righteous, not even one;
there is no one who understands;
there is no one who seeks God.
All have turned away,
they have together become worthless;
there is no one who does good,
not even one."
"Their throats are open graves;
their tongues practice deceit."
"The poison of vipers is on their lips."
"Their mouths are full of cursing and bitterness."
"Their feet are swift to shed blood;
ruin and misery mark their ways,
and the way of peace they do not know."
"There is no fear of God before their eyes."
(Romans 3:10-18)


Well…
Romans 4:3-8 suggests something else.  What we might call "imposed righteousness:"

What does Scripture say? "Abraham believed God, and it was credited to him as righteousness."
Now to the one who works, wages are not credited as a gift but as an obligation. However, to the one who does not work but trusts God who

justifies the ungodly, their faith is credited as righteousness. David says the same thing when he speaks of the blessedness of the one to whom God credits righteousness apart from works:

"Blessed are those
whose transgressions are forgiven,
whose sins are covered.
Blessed is the one
whose sin the Lord will never count against them."


We are sinners. But God has forgiven us. And he has declared us righteous.

Of course, all this criticism of the possibility of anyone being righteous fails to reckon with the obvious: as Christians, we have been declared righteous. By God. We are saved not by what we do but by what Jesus did. So, behavior has been eliminated from the equation altogether. Our righteousness is in Christ. When God looks at us, he sees Jesus, who already took the rap for our bad deeds. All our debts have been paid. Our credit is stellar. We are perfect.

And so, yes, it is the fact that the righteous do suffer. And in fact the Bible promises us that the righteous will suffer. So it shouldn't surprise us.

I mean, Peter wrote:

Dear friends, do not be surprised at the fiery ordeal that has come on you to test you, as though something strange were happening to you. (1 Peter 4:12)


We are elsewhere told to take up our cross and follow Jesus (Matthew 16:24). Taking up a cross does not seem like a happy prospect. Taking up a cross meant that you were on your way to be executed really, really soon.  It was a hard road, and nothing about it was good or pleasant.  It was nothing but suffering.  And it was going to end badly.

So "why do the righteous suffer" seems—and really is—an odd question, one that no one much asked.  Which, as I said last time, is why I say it is a modern issue, a modern question, an Enlightenment question, a question that has arisen because suffering has become increasingly unusual in our modern world.

I mean, think about it.  If you get a headache, you take a pain killer.  If you have a tooth ache, you go to the dentist; things that were major causes of everyday suffering simply don't exist for us anymore.  We would find it weird to have to *endure* pain; if it is hot, we put on the air; we have fans; our cars...ac and heat in cars is normal.  You didn't have that on foot or on horseback or camelback.  Even rich guys being carried in carriages didn't have that.  You feel like a snack, you have food: preserved, cold, good tasting.  You have coffee, tea, soda—no one had soda before the 1880s.  Cold beer?  Only if its wintertime and you left it outside.

I'd have died from my childhood illnesses if it weren't for the now rather primitive medical technology of the early 1960s.  There were no vaccines for the stuff that nearly killed me; now my children never had to endure measles, or mumps, or even chicken pox.

It is clear from a biblical and experiential standpoint: suffering is real.  And what is also real is that we are righteous, and God does not hold our sins against us.  Thus: it is not the case that there are no good people.  We have been made good in Christ.  And it is not the case that suffering is the result of us doing bad things: that is, it is simply not the case that bad things happen to bad people and good things to good people.

What does suffering tell us about God?  One very clear thing: it is not because of our sin.  Why?  *Because Jesus already suffered for that.*

What does suffering tell us about God?  We learn that God loves us: he tells us he does and he shows us he does.  Because God suffered for us.

We learn that suffering is part of the universe that God has put us into.  Suffering does not exclude our existence.  So, if our existence is compatible with suffering, why would we imagine God's existence isn't?  One very obvious thing we need to remember about suffering: God himself suffers.  We don't suffer it alone. He suffers with us.  He really does know our pain.  Suffering is as much a problem for God as it is for us.

If God loves us, if God is good, if God is powerful, why do the righteous suffer?  Well, if God loves himself, if God is good, and if God is powerful, why does HE suffer?

Suffering is not incompatible with our existence.  It is part of our existence.  Likewise, suffering is not incompatible with God's existence.  It is part of his existence.

It's not just free will (liberty), that has something to do with suffering.  Love also has something to do with suffering.

The whole point of this book is to provide an answer to suffering. Even so, it probably won't help much in the middle of torment. As we writhe in pain, all we want is for the pain to end. We don't care about philosophy, then.  But afterwards, when we have time to think, then we wouldn't mind an explanation.  A way of making sense of it all would be nice.

So.

Do you suppose there is one answer for everything and everyone?

Do we all take our coffee just the same?  Do we all like the same color cars?  The same kind of cars?  The same style of shoe?

Does one size really fit all?

So why do the righteous suffer?

You see, we like grand solutions, one size fits all.  We want to find a formula, a key to the problem that will answer it for us and give us a ten-part checklist that will be applicable to everyone. We seek a grand unified theory: an answer to everything.  And there is that, there really is.  But part of the solution to the problem as we see it is individual.

Most of her students do pretty well in class; the standard general curriculum works for them.  But others, due to learning disabilities, mental health issues, and other problems, struggle. So they get an IEP—an individualized educational program.  It is designed to focus on their unique needs and adjust the educational process to help them make it in school.

On the other end of the spectrum are the gifted.  They need individualized instruction to maximize their potential, too.

When I was a senior in high school back in the days before AP classes, I was in the advanced, honors English class.  This meant we looked at the classics, in depth.  But then there was me, and admittedly I am odd.  And my teacher recognized that and so while the rest of the honors class had to read one of Shakespeare's plays—Romeo and Juliet, again.  I had to read all of them and write papers on them.    And   then   when   we   studied   Henrik   Ibsen (Norwegian, 1906-1906), they just read *A Doll's House*.  I had to read all of his plays, and the plays of another, related playwright from the same time period, August Strindberg (Swedish, 1849-1912)—and write papers on each of them. They were both part of the naturalist movement in theatre and are the reason the plays are constructed the way they are today, how they look, and then that impacted how movies are done. Naturalistic works exposed the dark harshness of life, including poverty, racism, sex, prejudice, disease, prostitution, and filth; they are set in the real world, with everyday, ordinary speech forms and plausibility. They are very significant.   And so on; whatever the class had to do, I ended up doing more.  I even taught a couple of class sessions.

No matter what, in education, just as in other parts of our lives, we have to adjust it a bit for each person. Everyone is different.  Not everyone wants to eat kale for supper.

So, when we think about suffering, the Bible does provide some specific, explicit answers to the question of why?  God sometimes gives answers to individuals for their individual pain.  He just doesn't bother to give an obvious answer to life the universe and everything.

So, Joseph went through the wringer, and so did is dad, Jacob.  Jacob complained and announced in Genesis 42 after recounting his long list of troubles that "Everything is against me."  Meanwhile, Joseph had been sold into slavery by his own half-brothers, falsely accused of a crime, and tossed into prison for years.

But of course it worked out; the suffering ended for both of them.  And why did Jacob and Joseph suffer?  What was the reason for their pain?  Joseph tells his brothers the answer in Genesis 50:19-20:

> "Don't be afraid. Am I in the place of God? You
> intended to harm me, but God intended it for good
> to accomplish what is now being done, the saving
> of many lives."

Why did all the awful things happen to Job?
To prove a point with Satan regarding the question of why the righteous serve God.

One day Jesus and his disciples came upon a man who had been blind from birth (John 9:1-3). His disciples had a question for Jesus:

"Rabbi, who sinned, this man or his parents, that he was born blind?"

And Jesus gave them an answer for that individual's hard life of suffering for forty years:

"Neither this man nor his parents sinned," said Jesus, "but this happened so that the works of God might be displayed in him."

So this man was miserable for forty years so that Jesus could show up one day and demonstrate the power of God.

It's an answer.

Notice that in all three cases, the answers are specific, for the specific individual's involved. The answers are not universal, not the answer to life, the universe and everything.

When Peter caught a fish and yanked a couple of coins from its mouth to pay the temple tax is that story then a universal formula for how to pay your taxes?

> "But so that we may not cause offense, go to the lake and throw out your line. Take the first fish you catch; open its mouth and you will find a four-drachma coin. Take it and give it to them for my tax and yours." (Matthew 17:27)

Or are these stories more universal than we think?

Perhaps we can tease out something universal from it: trusting God, obeying him—for the tax thing. And for the others: the knowledge that there are reasons for what happens. At least there were reasons for Jacob, Joseph, Job and the man born blind. Perhaps we can have hope there is an answer for all of us, too, for everything we go through.

In Romans 14:19-23 Paul explains that things are not always the same for everyone, even when it comes to questions of morality and ethics:

> Let us therefore make every effort to do what leads to peace and to mutual edification. Do not destroy the work of God for the sake of food. All food is clean, but it is wrong for a person to eat anything that causes someone else to stumble. It is better not to eat meat or drink wine or to do anything else that will cause your brother or sister to fall.

> So whatever you believe about these things keep between yourself and God. Blessed is the one who does not condemn himself by what he approves. But whoever has doubts is condemned if they eat, because their eating is not from faith; and everything that does not come from faith is sin.

And so if things are sometimes individual, if there really is just "truth for me" then what are we to do with this issue of suffering?   Is it all a waste of time to talk about it?  The author of Ecclesiastes argues that life has no meaning; he affirms it is ultimately absurd, and pointless, and he believes that any meaning comes from an individual's own decision—*assuming* that God doesn't care to interact with his creatures and has not bothered to reveal himself to us.

See, the ultimate point—the non-absurdity—of the book of Ecclesiastes is that it demonstrates the need for something like the Bible in the first place.  The author is going to explain that if all we had to go on was what we can figure out from life the universe and everything, then God is unknowable, the meaning to life is unknowable, and life is thus obviously absurd and pointless. *"Meaningless"* Ecclesiastes' author would—and does—argue.

And he sets it all up for us in the very beginning of his philosophic treatise, his essay on life as something absurd.

So, some additional preliminaries now to help us find our way through this dark forest, this gloomy jungle of an essay, this valley of the shadow of death.

How do we learn about God? That is, what is the source for information about him? If God exists, then he should, in some way, be accessible. We should be able to find out things about him. But how? One way is called "general revelation."

General revelation refers to that information that comes from the universe around us and from history (see Psalm 19:1-6, Romans 1:19-20, Psalm 8:13, Isaiah 40:12-14, 26, Acts 14:15-17, 17:24- 28). It reveals, or informs us on such matters as the wisdom, power, and glory of God (Romans 1:20). But general revelation also gives us darkness.

It gives us pain, and suffering. Dr. McCoy in the first of the new Star Trek movies commented about space that "Space is disease and danger wrapped in darkness and silence."

Which is of course an introduction to Dr. McCoy's outlook on life, but also serves as a bit of what life—general revelation—gives us. History is an endless landscape of disease, and death, of war and famine, of heartache and unjust pain, and just the mild grumpiness that confronts us in any given day: the minor setbacks, the petty injustices and disappointments.

Voltaire's work *Candide* was inspired by a number of things. Most prominently, he was reacting to the publication of Leibniz's "Monadology," a short metaphysical treatise. He also was affected by the Seven Years' War and by the 1755 Lisbon earthquake. Both of the latter catastrophes are frequently referred to in *Candide* and are cited by scholars as reasons for its composition. The 1755 Lisbon earthquake, tsunami, and resulting fires on All

Saints' Day, had a strong influence on theologians of the day and on Voltaire, who was himself disillusioned by them. The earthquake had an especially large effect on the contemporary doctrine of optimism, a philosophical system which some argued implied that such horrific events should not occur. Optimism was founded on the theodicy of Gottfried Wilhelm Leibniz. It argues that all is for the best because God is a benevolent deity. This concept is often put into the form, "all is for the best in the best of all possible worlds." Philosophers had trouble fitting the horrors of this earthquake into such an optimistic view of reality.

Voltaire actively rejected Leibnizian optimism after the natural disaster, convinced that if this were the best possible world, it should surely be better than it is. In Candide, Voltaire attacks this optimist belief. He makes use of the Lisbon earthquake to argue this point, sarcastically describing the catastrophe as one of the most horrible disasters "in the best of all possible worlds."

General revelation, like Special revelation is sufficient, not complete or exhaustive. It does not tell us everything there is to know about God or the universe. Christian theologians will be quick to point out that the Bible, an example of special revelation, has serious limitations. It does not even attempt to answer all the questions we might have about God.

As interested as we are in how old the universe is and exactly how it came to be, those were not questions that the biblical writers tried to answer. We are very curious about the devil, what motivates him, where he came from. The biblical authors never attempted to answer either of those modern questions, either. The Bible does not provide medical or scientific information; it does not offer a cure for cancer or bipolar disorder; it does not discuss how one might prevent or cure infections. There is nothing within its pages about dark matter, dark energy, or whether string theory is ever going to be testable.  It offers no theories regarding quantum gravity.  Neither will a reader find solutions for poverty or any discussions regarding what so focuses our attentions regarding the latest issues in politics or who to vote for or against.  There is not a bit of information in the Bible about how to repair a carburetor or how to get the sound to work on one's cellphone.  The Bible does not offer an answer to how best to govern a nation or what sort of economic policies are preferable.  It gives us no solutions for poverty or homelessness, or how to stop oppression, aggression, or war. There are no hidden cures for cancer or mental illness in the pages of the Bible.

Thus, general revelation has its role to play, just as special revelation does.  But both are only limited vessels of information, neither able to offer complete guidance or answers to every possible conundrum.  Those who tell you that they know the answers for every problem, especially the ones that so vex and concern you, are just trying to sell you something or get control over you.

And yet, I believe that we can learn an answer to the question that Voltaire and Leibniz argue with one another about.  And it is a combination of both scripture—special revelation—and general revelation—life—that can help us find a way to both the specific, individual answer we seek, and the more general, universal—answer for everything answer—that we want as well.

So, when we look at the answers given in Genesis—about why Jacob and Joseph suffered—or in Job—why Job suffered—or the man born blind—why he suffered.  What do their individual answers have in common?

- The Power of Saving lives (Joseph and Jacob)
- The Power of Love (Job: why do the righteous be righteous?)
- The Power of God (why this individual suffered blindness)

In all cases, there is a greater good that results from the problem, the suffering.  This seems inherent in the issue, when we consider the issue of liberty; that is, it would seem that liberty is more important than peace, prosperity, harmony, everyone being good all the time; liberty—the freedom to choose (in the case of Adam and Eve with the tree of the knowledge of good and evil) is the greater good than simply not making the choice to disobey in the first place.

In the movie *Saving Private Ryan*, the movie is focused on finding one particular soldier and bringing him home because he is the lone surviving son; his brothers have all been killed and the idea of an entire family being wiped out by combat is unacceptable to the military.

And so the question of the story is obviously one of suffering.  And the question is also: what is the life of this one soldier worth?  How many other soldiers must die in the attempt to find and save him?

The needs of the one, to quote from Star Trek III, outweigh the needs of the many?

Jesus told a parable:

> "What do you think? If a man owns a hundred sheep, and one of them wanders away, will he not leave the ninety-nine on the hills and go to look for the one that wandered off? And if he finds it, truly I tell you, he is happier about that one sheep than about the ninety-nine that did not wander off. In the same way your Father in heaven is not willing that any of these little ones should perish. (Matthew 18:12-14)

Leave the 99 and find the 1.

Or do the needs of the many outweigh the needs of the one? As Spock would argue.

Or as we see in the last of the Harry Potter novels, with Dumbledore and Grindelwald in their youth and the declaration, "for the greater good." What is needed for the greater good? Is that a reasonable argument? To weigh in the balance the different levels of suffering, the amount of suffering, and decide that the deaths of these thousands is worthwhile in this war because it saves the lives of millions? Or to put it in the harsh terms of a tyrant, you can't have an omelet without breaking some eggs? Or, as Joseph Stalin said, the death of one is a tragedy, but the death of a million is statistics.

Do we justify God, explain suffering, in terms of eggs and statistics? Somehow the suffering of the millions in wars, disease, and holocaust are for the greater good of...liberty? Or to bring in the kingdom? Or, to use Joseph's words "so that many lives will be saved?"

Somehow the answer seems to be yes, even though emotionally it feels...inadequate...

And so we get to the third L, the Leftovers (remember, logic, liberty, leftovers).

The need for imperfections in order for existence at all, and in order to bring about ultimate goodness and even perfection.

Sometimes we know exactly why we are suffering.

And we make a decision, in the midst of our pain, as to whether we think it is worth it. The reasons we continue in our misery can be complicated.

Perhaps you were forced by your parents to learn to play the piano; you didn't really want to do it, but they made you. And you kept at it because you didn't want the greater pain of being punished, or their disappointment? Or maybe you came to appreciate the value of knowing how to play an instrument and accepted the drudgery as a reasonable price to pay?

If we were played football, or baseball, basketball or did track or swimming, we endured the practices, the strenuous exercise.  Those who make it to the Olympics go through a lot of hard work, a lot of pain, a lot of inconvenience and discomfort to get there.  The struggle is real.

Going to school was not always pleasant, it was not always fun; certainly not as enjoyable as spring break or summers off.  But we went, we did papers, we did homework, we studied into the night.  We did it all because we wanted to graduate, because we knew we needed to do well to get the job we wanted later, or because we wanted to impress someone, or please our parents, or avoid our parents' wrath.  Perhaps we persevered only because it was the lesser of evils.

Since my parents paid for my undergraduate education, including room and board, I treated it as if it were my job, on top of the satisfaction I got from learning, and the innate desire I had to succeed.  But it wasn't always pleasant.  I lost a lot of sleep; I didn't go out and socialize as much as I otherwise might have.

My parents did not pay for my graduate work.  I had to take care of that myself. And so I worked long hours, went without sleep, focused on a difficult major.  It was a lot of "suffering" and it was all self-inflicted.  I burned myself out just so I could learn the languages I wanted to learn and get the degree I wanted.  Those things, for me, made the years of only four-hour-a-night sleep worth it to me.  I saw a purpose, a use, a value to my misery.

Going to work, being at work: we don't do it because it is fun, at least not most of the time.  We do it for the weekends.  We do it because we need the money.  We put up with it, and endure the pain, because we know we have to.  The benefits of work outweigh the pain of it.

As I pointed out earlier, life in general is like an IEP for students with special needs.  Our suffering is individual, and often the explanation for our suffering is just as individual.  But we see an answer, most of the time in the middle of the common day-to-day suffering we put up with: we know precisely why it is happening and we accept it, perhaps even rejoice in the opportunity for the pain.

In the book of Acts, we can read about how the apostles were arrested:

> "The apostles were brought in and made to appear before the Sanhedrin to be questioned by the high priest. 'We gave you strict orders not to teach in this name,' he said. 'Yet you have filled Jerusalem with your teaching and are determined to make us guilty of this man's blood.'
>
> "Peter and the other apostles replied: 'We must obey God rather than human beings! The God of our ancestors raised Jesus from the dead—whom you killed by hanging him on a cross. God exalted him to his own right hand as Prince and Savior that he might bring Israel to repentance and forgive their sins. We are witnesses of these things, and so is the Holy Spirit, whom God has given to those who obey him.'" (Acts 5:27-32)

Then the apostles were flogged and ordered to shut up about Jesus.

How did they respond to their pain?

> "The apostles left the Sanhedrin, rejoicing because they had been counted worthy of suffering disgrace for the Name. Day after day, in the temple courts and from house to house, they never stopped teaching and proclaiming the good news that Jesus is the Messiah." (Acts 5:41-42)

They suffered. They accepted the discomfort. And they knew why they were suffering. For them, it was worth it.

What are some universal truths can we get from individual pain?  If nothing else, that suffering indeed can have meaning and value.

But Ecclesiastes 1:1-11 argues that everything is meaningless and seems to run counter to the idea that suffering—or really anything about life—gives us meaning or purpose.

> The words of the Teacher, son of David, king in
> Jerusalem:
>  "Meaningless! Meaningless!"
> says the Teacher.
> "Utterly meaningless!
> Everything is meaningless."
> What do people gain from all their labors
> at which they toil under the sun?
>  Generations come and generations go,
> but the earth remains forever.
>  The sun rises and the sun sets,
> and hurries back to where it rises.
>  The wind blows to the south
> and turns to the north;
> round and round it goes,
> ever returning on its course.
>  All streams flow into the sea,
> yet the sea is never full.
> To the place the streams come from,
> there they return again.
>  All things are wearisome,
> more than one can say.
> The eye never has enough of seeing,
> nor the ear its fill of hearing.
> What has been will be again,
> what has been done will be done again;
> there is nothing new under the sun.
>  Is there anything of which one can say,

"Look! This is something new"?
It was here already, long ago;
it was here before our time.
 No one remembers the former generations,
and even those yet to come
will not be remembered
by those who follow them.

Tellingly, the happier one feels, the more meaningful life characteristically seems. Thus no one says, "I feel blissfully happy, but my life feels meaningless." Perhaps compare how mania is associated with an indiscriminately heightened sense of significance. Conversely, low mood is bound up with a pervasive sense of emptiness and a lack of motivation, shading into the nihilistic despair of severe depression.

Is suffering worth it?  Which brings us to the ultimate question:

Is non-existing then preferable to existing?

God would answer no.  And therefore we exist.

Not all would agree, of course.  Going back to the *Hitchhiker' Guide,* we return to that quote regarding the creation of the universe, that "many believe this was a bad idea."  Antinatalism is a philosophical position that argues that coming into existence was inherently bad because life perpetuates suffering.  David Benatar in 2006 published a book entitled *Better Never to Have Been: the harm of coming into existence.*

Crudely, life is suffering, as the Gautama Buddha might say.

Logically, the existence of suffering does not exclude the existence of God, not only because it is a non-sequitur for the question, but because God himself suffers, too.  In thinking about suffering, it too often is portrayed as if it is something unique to people, or to life on earth.  It includes God.  God suffers. He has, by creating us, chosen to suffer.

He thinks it is worth it for him to suffer with us, so that we can exist.

Liberty is the greatest good; liberty is better, more important than, just raw force. This is what it comes down to: if morality is most important, then that means someone will force obedience, and if obedience really is then the most critical thing, then power is pre-eminent. Making things the way they need to be. Might makes right? Does it? Is totalitarianism the answer? Do we like being told we have to be a certain way? You must eat your liver and onions because it is good for you! You cannot have a straw. Plastic bags are a no-no. You can't say that!

If you insist on order and absolute morality, then power is all that matters and we are robots with no choices or free will. If you allow choice, if you allow freedom: bad things will happen. If the universe as a whole is designed to have free creatures in it, that means that randomness is part of it. As the author of Ecclesiastes tells us, "time and chance happen to all."

God thought the suffering that comes with freedom, the *imperfection* of freedom was better than totalitarianism.

Leftovers: imperfection is not bad; imperfection makes existence possible. Asymmetries: it is statistical, and it is hard, but it is reality and makes reality possible. So the ultimate question of life, the universe and everything is not, why is there suffering, but instead, why is there existence? Is existence worth it?

The ultimate question of life, the universe and everything is not why do the righteous suffer? That is not the real question at all.

God promised us that we would suffer:

> "If the world hates you, keep in mind that it hated me first. If you belonged to the world, it would love you as its own. As it is, you do not belong to the world, but I have chosen you out of

the world. That is why the world hates you. Remember what I told you: 'A servant is not greater than his master.' If they persecuted me, they will persecute you also. If they obeyed my teaching, they will obey yours also. They will treat you this way because of my name, for they do not know the one who sent me. (John 15:18-21)

And

"I have told you these things, so that in me you may have peace. In this world you will have trouble. But take heart! I have overcome the world." (John 16:33)

We are told to take up our cross.

Then he said to them all: "Whoever wants to be my disciple must deny themselves and take up their cross daily and follow me. (Luke 9:23)

We are told to join in the sufferings of Christ:

Now if we are children, then we are heirs—heirs of God and co-heirs with Christ, if indeed we share in his sufferings in order that we may also share in his glory. (Romans 8:17)

For just as we share abundantly in the sufferings of Christ, so also our comfort abounds through Christ. (2 Corinthians 1:5)

For it has been granted to you on behalf of Christ not only to believe in him, but also to suffer for him, (Philippians 1:29)

I want to know Christ—yes, to know the power of his resurrection and participation in his sufferings, becoming like him in his death, (Philippians 3:10)

We should not be surprised:

Dear friends, do not be surprised at the fiery ordeal that has come on you to test you, as though something strange were happening to you. (1 Peter 4:12)

Remember: God suffers too, not just us. When he decided to create the universe, he knew that there would be suffering and he knew that he would suffer himself more than we can imagine. He decided not that your suffering or my suffering made existence worthwhile. It was more than that. He decided his own suffering still made existence worthwhile.

Why do we suffer? Why does God suffer? Now the mechanism. We suffer because we love. God suffers because he IS love. Without love—whether love of self, or love of others—there would be no suffering.

We suffer when we are in pain. Why? Because we love ourselves. We suffer when others suffer. Why? Because we love ourselves.

And yet suffering is not all that we do in life. It is a part of life, but it is not of what life consists. The Buddha said that "life is suffering." I don't think so. Suffering is merely a *part* of life. But there is more to it than that…or else, why would we continue to exist? Why would we struggle and overcome? The cancer sufferer does not just lie down peacefully and die. She fights, she suffers through the chemo and radiation or immunotherapy and hopes and often does beat the disease. She triumphs over the pain, the agony, the suffering. We encourage people with the thought against suicide: don't use a permanent solution to solve a temporary problem.  Where there is life, there is hope, we say.  Every creature on earth rages against the darkness, rages against the dying of the light, rages against death.  Dylan Thomas wrote a poem, *Do Not Go Gentle* which begins:

> Do not go gentle into that good night,
> Old age should burn and rave at close of day;
> Rage, rage against the dying of the light.

Is life worthwhile?  Is suffering worthwhile?
Is *love* worthwhile?
That is the fourth L—which I seem to have forgotten to label explicitly until now, but it is there, nonetheless. Inescapably.  God is love, we are told by the apostle John in his first letter. We know the verses.  There's even an old Christian song from the seventies that made use of John's words:

> Dear friends, let us love one another, for love comes from God. Everyone who loves has been born of God and knows God. Whoever does not love does not know God, because God is love. (1 John 4:7-8)

It is not just that God loves; it is more profound than that.  He *is* love.

And God's existence is worthwhile.  And God not only suffers in himself, because he loves himself, he suffers for us, because he loves us.  He suffers with us.  And we, as Christians, join in his sufferings.  Suffering motivates us: it motivates us to fight, to endure, to rage, and to love.

The question is simply this: is existence worthwhile?
Life's tenacity argues it is.
And that is the real question, not why is there suffering, but, will it stop us?  Will we not struggle against

it?  Will we not continue to love and be loved?  Is it not all worth it in the end?

The more you love, the more you feel loved—and the less suffering hurts.

So is existence worthwhile?

We suffer. Most assuredly.

But our continued, and by our, I mean not just humans, but *all* of life's abundance and resilience insists and shouts that it is worthwhile.  Every day we arise, every day we breathe, every day that we continue to reproduce and keep going despite the pain demonstrates that it is worth it. The abundance of life, our continuing existence over eons of history, demonstrates that we are convinced that we matter, and that life and existence matter, and that it is all worthwhile.

That we live at all, and have children, and rescue and nurture, and cherish demonstrates that we think that it all matters, that it all has meaning, and that yes, existence is worth it.

We live the answer when we get up each day and start over again, no matter what.

The question is not why do we suffer, but why do we endure?

Why? Because we have to!

www.ingramcontent.com/pod-product-compliance
Lightning Source LLC
Chambersburg PA
CBHW072223150726
48002CB00005B/1937